TENNESSEE CHICKEN:

REAL LIFE STORIES OF AN ORPHAN FROM EAST TENNESSEE

BY: EMMETT DODSON & WILL DODSON

Text copyright ©2013

Emmett Dodson & Will Dodson

All Rights Reserved

Dedicated to our wives Karen & Katy Dodson

Without their love, neither author would have survived

"So Chick, you always say you're half Cherokee, what's the other half?"

"Well, I'm half Cherokee and half magician"

"What do you mean half magician?"

"Well my momma was a Cherokee and my daddy must have been a magician because when he found out she was pregnant with me, he disappeared and they never found him again!"

Foreword

"My momma left me in Washington D.C. when I was five years old. Thank God abortion wasn't legal back then because I wouldn't have had the privilege of meeting my wife, Karen, and ending up with one of the greatest heroes I've ever known…my son. With all that said, I am going to start telling you what I did when I was young and what I think of America as it is today. We were raised years ago to believe in the flag, believe in this country and when duty called, right or wrong, the country was first. You should respect your servicemen, because there is no greater gift you can give to mankind than your life. If you give your life, you give all you can give and with all that said, I will begin to tell my story."

--Emmett "Tennessee Chicken" Dodson

Preface

A half Cherokee and half something or another, my father was born in Kingsport, Tennessee in 1931. His mother was Cherokee, but more than that she liked to drink and have a good time. She bounced around East Tennessee and eventually landed in Washington D.C. living on Indian welfare at the time. Dad said they were good at midnight moves and whenever rent came due his mother would take him to the next place to live. Dad was a small child during these times and he experienced poverty at the very definition. Poverty doesn't pick a particular race, age, religion, creed or geographic location; it hurts all it inflicts until they are able to rise out of it. Dad was abandoned by his mother in D.C., left on a boarding room bed all alone. An African-American woman by the name of "Minnie," took care of the building and found my Dad all alone and crying. Dad called her "Aunt Minnie." Aunt Minnie took my Dad to live with her and her eight children, in Washington D.C. for awhile. Although his birth mother left him, for the time being, Aunt Minnie did not and treated him as if he were one of her own. Dad said he was grateful that abortion wasn't legal back then, because, if it was, he wouldn't have made it. My father lived an adventurous life. For an orphan, who didn't have a chance in Hell to make it, he did it and he did it with a smile. Yes, he saw many hard times. Nothing like we can imagine in this day and age. If anyone wanted to know tough times they should have been born in East Tennessee in 1931. It just doesn't get any rougher. However, that is not the point of this epic book. The point is to remember that Someone is always watching over you, Someone is walking beside you and leading you through your own individual journey, your own set of adventures. The following are short stories of my Dad's life, also known as "Tennessee Chicken" and with a name like that, well reader; you've just got to believe every single word!

--Will Dodson

From Kingsport to Lenoir City by Will Dodson

As stated earlier, as a small child, my Dad moved from Kingsport, Tennessee to Washington D.C. with his mother in the 1930s. They lived there, jumping from different rentals, having many "midnight moves." Dad's mother had a boyfriend named Emmett. Emmett painted houses for money during the day and drank and fought during the night. His nocturnal activities eventually put him in jail for a period of time and my Dad's mother eventually left D.C., but without Dad. The caretaker of the building, which Dad was left in, was named Minnie. "Aunt Minnie," as Dad called her, took him to live with her in her small home with her eight children in D.C. "Aunt Minnie" loved my Dad and treated him as one of her own. "Aunt Minnie" was the closet resemblance of a real mother my Dad had and he loved her dearly. Eventually, Emmett got out of jail and, seeing that his girlfriend had abandoned my Dad, decided he would take Dad back to Lenoir City, Tennessee with him. That would be the last time my Dad would ever see "Aunt Minnie" but he would never forget her love. Dad would call all of Emmett's family his own for a while, including his foster uncles and granny, who you will hear more about later in this book.

Lenoir City is a small town in East Tennessee, located in Loudon County and situated on the Tennessee River. Even today it remains a small rural town in a very beautiful setting. The Tennessee Valley Authority, established in the 1930s would change the local economy and the Tennessee River with the construction of the Fort Loudon Dam. Dad's mother came back and forth in his life but never stayed with him for any long period of time. The following set of stories happened between Dad's time in D.C. and in Lenoir City during the Great Depression.

Meeting Mrs. Roosevelt

I guess the reason my Momma carried me to Washington D.C. was for the perks, the "give me's." We had to be on relief or something. We were always getting these big goodie bags. We were in a theatre around Christmas, and Eleanor Roosevelt was handing out these big duffle bags with all kinds of food and toys in them. She handed one to my Momma that had a sailboat in it. She patted me on the head and they took a picture of it and it came out in one of the papers in Washington D.C. I think I know the reason that they took me. Well you talk about ugly, son, I was ugly! I had an eye out of line that looked straight out and one that looked straight up. I was pitiful looking. I had a set of little ole skinny legs and looked like I hadn't eaten anything in a year, which I probably hadn't! It wasn't hard to get a bag when you had a young'n that looked like that!

Chicken Stompin'

Well reader…first of all everybody talks about the good ole days. The good ole days were good for some people! If you had a lot of money and a big farm or owned a meat market or something, the good ole days were good. But on our end, they weren't!

My wife once told me a story about driving with her Dad as a kid. I don't know how he got a car back then but she was saying that they used to go riding on Sunday out in the country. If they could find hickory nuts or anything to eat, they would eat it. If they saw a chicken run across the street, he would try to swerve to hit it for dinner. Well, I was brought back to a little old city called Lenoir City. It's kind of hard to stomp a chicken when you see it run across the road because we sure didn't have any cars during that time! Have you ever tried to stomp a chicken? It doesn't matter how many folks you have aiming at that chicken, you won't do it. Trust me, I tried many times and failed many times. Chickens might be stupid, but they sure can move. They stay suspicious!

I don't know how East Tennessee ever made it. Times were rough before the Second World War. I would see grown men crying because they couldn't feed their families. In fact, I saw my foster uncle cry many times because he couldn't feed his kids.

Poor Folks

I laughed at a friend of mine the other day. She said something happened in New York, where she was from, and when they got to looking through the old papers where her momma and them had bought the house, on a bill it had written on it "poor folks." She said they didn't realize they were poor. Well, buddy, up there in those mountains we knew we were poor and if it hadn't been for Roosevelt, the relief and the yellow grits, I'm not so sure we would have been here, we would have been aborted anyway! Roosevelt started the WPA and CC Camp. You would have thought that they hit the lottery back then because a man could earn a dollar a day. A dollar could get you a lot of things back then. Seven dollars would fill up the back of a truck with groceries. You bought everything like sugar, coffee, flour, and you could even buy a twenty-five pound sack of lard for biscuits. Speaking of which, it was rare to get light bread. Well, when we went to school they would put lard on a biscuit and a little salt on it for flavor. You would carry a little lard bucket, like those pound lard buckets, carry that for a lunch bucket and it tasted pretty good, because we were really hungry.

I will never forget when I started school in Lenoir City, this one boy's momma owned a beauty shop and I reckon back then, even when times were tough, women still paid to get their hair done. Well anyways, this boy would bring those sandwiches to school, with light bread and baloney. I would sit there and want that light bread and not knowing that the biscuit I had was ten times better than that light bread. It was awful to sit there and watch a fella eat a light bread and baloney sandwich and you were sitting there eating a biscuit with lard on it!

By the way, the grandmother in my foster family could take yellow grits and corn meal and she could make corn dumplings, so we got by. Folks had a lot of pride back then. Everybody thinks that you have to have a whole lot of money to be rich. Well we feel like we are rich today. Look at all the food we have today. You can run down to the store anytime and buy food, open any cabinet and food is there. My wife always believed in having a lot of food. We eat anything we want today. You can run down to these fast food places and get a hamburger with fries and you get more than you can eat. They do that everywhere, even at them Mexican restaurants. Hell when you get done, you leave half of what you get. We can sit down, and eat a steak, and we remember the days when, boy, wouldn't I have loved to have had this. That one steak could have fed the entire family as hungry as we were! It's great to be American.

The people today are better off than they ever have been. Folks just need to put things in perspective.

The Applecart

Now as far as some of the stuff I've done, I eventually went to the Tennessee Industrial School (TIS), now called the Tennessee Preparatory School. I got sent out there because I was on the street after I had run away from different foster families in East Tennessee.

Living on the street, I did a lot of things I shouldn't have done. When you are street, that's all you know. I got a job in this store during the War. Everything was rationed on account of the War. You couldn't get sugar, lard, pineapples, soap powder, nothing. Me and this ole boy were working one day in the store; I guess they called us sack boys. We did everything. When a load of that Dove or Oxydol soap powder came in, we were scared we would get trampled. Instead of carrying it down and putting it up on the shelf, we just carried it to the balcony, where the owner stored items. We would drop it over and people would almost kill each other trying to get it. So, one day, I ain't going to tell you the boy's name, I'll just call him the owner. The owner told us, "When ya'll get off, I want you to go by my house." He had some old pear trees in his yard. The rotten pears draw bees and things. Well he wanted us to clean them up. He had a blind horse and a wagon. He said, "I want you all to clean up these pears and haul them off." He said there were a bunch of empty baskets in his basement. It was a great big ole house. He said, "When you rake those pears up, you can put them in there and haul them off." We got over there and started raking those pears and got them all piled up. There were a mess of them. We went inside the house to get the baskets to put those pears in and boy did we hit it! It was like walking into Fort Knox. That fella had all kinds of stuff stored in there! He had stuff you couldn't get. Soap powders, pineapples, lard. He had cigarettes.

You couldn't get cigarettes back then. He was hoarding it and that was against Federal Law, and we knew it. I hate to tell this, but we did it anyway. We loaded those baskets full of goodies and we topped them with the old pears and took off. Well, needless to say...we got fired. He couldn't turn us in because what he did would have landed him in the penitentiary. It was funny. We bought old long coats and we were standing at the ends of town and somebody would come by and we would say, "Hey Buddy, you wanna buy a pack of cigarettes?" Nobody asked where we got them. They were buying things like crazy. We were selling cigarettes 50 cents a pack. He would ride along with that wagon, and I would jump off and knock on the door and a woman would come to the door and I would ask, "Lady would you like to buy a box of Dove soap?" Nobody cared, they just bought! They didn't ask where we got it. We made a pile of money doing this. Believe me! So we took off to Florida. We had a pretty good time. I'm sorry to have to tell about it, but that's just the way it was. That was just one of the things we did together before I went to work for that store, I knew the boy with the blind mule because of another something I did in the next story!

The Lord Will Strike Thee Down

Before I went to work for that store, I knew the boy with the blind mule because, a year before that, I was walking along and I went by this house that had green apples on the ground. I looked over and saw these green apples lying all over the ground. I just walked over and picked up a couple of those apples. This fella came out, who happened to be a preacher. He reached up and pulled a limb off the tree, looked like he got half the tree, but I reckon it was just a switch. He liked to beat me to death for stealing apples and I said, "Hell, I didn't steal no apples, just picked up the one that fell off the tree and ate it." He was so mean and got so mad about it, I thought, fooey on you. From that day on, I didn't have much damn use for preachers. I told him, "I was hungry, the reason I ate that damned apple." The more I argued with him, the more he whooped. So I just shut up, and took a whooping. When he was done, I went and told this boy with the blind horse. We were pretty good friends. Here we went that night. I don't know how many damned trees that preacher had. That guy had quite a lot of trees and they did have some mighty fine apples. Me and that friend brought that mule. We sat there all night, and sawed every single one of those trees with a handsaw, and we took a bunch of those apples. I don't know what ever happened to that fella because we went separate ways. If anybody could get into trouble, I could. It wasn't hard for me. I had a knack for it.

Hot Dog!

Before World War II, you could go to the movie in Lenoir City. If you were under 12 years old, you could get in free. After that, you would have to pay 10 cents admission. Well, they had series like Buck Rogers or Flash Gordon. You would also get the news that went on for the week. Right next to the movie theatre, they had a Rexall drugstore. There was a window where you could pull the top down, and split the hotdogs, and put the hotdog and bun on there. They would cook and it would smell great. I would stand there and watch and my mouth would just water! When they opened up the facility at Oak Ridge, well, my foster cousin, Virginia, got a job there. She worked in the canteen. She came home with the very first check she had made, and she was so tickled with it that she started handing out money. She gave me a $5 bill. I thought *Lord Have*

Mercy! I was told I could spend it anyway I wanted. I got up Saturday morning and headed into town. We lived on 8th Street, and I stopped at the Five and Dime and got a quarter's worth of candy. They had chocolate covered orange slices and coconut kisses. Then, I went down to Rexall. For some reason, they had hotdogs two for a nickel. I got 35 cents worth of hotdogs. The guy was laughing at me as he fixed them. I got 14 hot dogs, a bag of candy, and two big orange drinks. I ate all of it and watched two movies. Well, when I got home that night I almost died. They threw me on the three sixes. That was a type of medicine they gave you back then. That was the way they cleaned you out. I went a long time before I ate any more hotdogs.

Dry Runs

They used to have an evergreen ointment for sore muscles. They called it "Atomic Bomb" after the War broke out.

Well, my foster grandma had a habit of keeping a slop jar under the bed. She would get up and think she was going to use it and all she would do was pass gas and wouldn't do anything. Then she would make me take it out and rinse it, and take it up to the outhouse - like it was full of something. It made me mad to have to get up in the middle of the night to empty an empty slop jar. I don't know why I did it but I did. I got a hold of some of that "Atomic Bomb" and I thought; I am going to fix her. I wrapped it around the edge of the slop jar and put the lid back on and slid it under the bed. Sure enough, "Grandma" got up and she sat on that pot. Well that wasn't a dry run! At that point, I got tickled about it and of course, got caught. They liked to beat me to death. I've never been whooped so hard in my life. They would whoop me, take time from whooping me and rest and whoop me some more! You can bet one thing, after grandma healed, she never had me jump up and do any of those dry runs again!

Mountain Folk Medicine

When I was little I had a pit bull as a pet and loved him to death. Well, one day I went to feed him and I saw him crouch and luckily I happened to drop my head down and my chin. As he lunged for my neck, he sunk his teeth into my upper lip instead. I still have the scars from it today but my mustache covers it up. Well, my uncle shot him right after that and I had begged him not to kill him but there wasn't any sense in it if he had turned on me like that. They are good dogs until they turn on you and you never know when that day will come. I can shoot a bulldog without even thinking about it because I am scared of it!

If the dog had been rabid that would have been all it was for me. They would have dug a hole and put me in it. They rushed me in the house and my granny told me to hold my breath and she dunked my head in a batch of kerosene. It was sore for a while after that. We didn't have health insurance and couldn't run down to the doctor back then. She used kerosene to cure everything. It would stop bleeding and take care of any skin problems. My granny used to soak her feet in it. Well as kids we didn't wear shoes in the springtime or summer time; you saved shoes for the winter. As kids, we were always getting nails in our feet. A nail is going to hurt when it goes plum through your foot. People would tear a board off something and wouldn't bend the nail just throw it off to the side. So when you played outside barefoot you were bound to get a nail in your foot. Kerosene would kill the pain and help it seal up.

Speaking of shoes I never had a new pair of shoes. I was third in line in whatever family I was in. I was never number one. Number one got the new shoes and after they were done if you were next in line and they fit you, then you would get them. Everything I got was second handed, even the bathwater. For the longest time when I took a bath I was second or third in the tub. We had to draw the water and heat it on the stove to take a hot bath. Usually we would just bathe in the creek when we could.

My granny had corn cob pipes and, the way she would cure them out and fix them, they looked like a store bought pipe. She would use cane. Cane was everywhere. She would get the small canes and make pipes. They wouldn't be little bitty corn cob pipes, they would be big ole long pipes. She grew something she called loco weed. It didn't smell like marijuana but it had the same effect. She would pick it and put it in a pillow slip. Her and the family would get to smoking that stuff and get friendly and happy. I don't know what they used to munch on after they smoked the loco weed because we didn't even have enough to eat three square meals. They must have been the hungriest and happiest people in the world. You couldn't sit there and eat donuts and tater chips and all that stuff back then! Only thing we had was yellow grits, gravy and biscuits. I guess the munchies were out on the loco weed.

Good for the Goose, Good for the Gander

After things got a little better and the Works Progress Administration came into effect, people started working again and they started to have a little money.

My foster uncle Oliver and foster uncle Philip got a bunch of chickens and kept them in a little pen. We would gather the eggs. I had the job of going in and feeding the chickens and watering them. We had a hydrant in the yard we used for water. We didn't have a hydrant in the house or anything so you had to go outside to get your water. Well, Uncle Oliver had a great big ole goose. I was small and that goose was taller than me. He knew I was scared of him. I would go in there and that goose would peck me on the top of my head. My head was sore as a boil. They thought it was funny. They would laugh and I would run all over that place with that goose popping me on the top of the head. One day I didn't feel well and they made me go in there and feed the chickens and I had to draw water and pour it in there in the trough. Well here came that ole goose. I was trying to hurry and get everything done before he spotted me. He came along and hit me two times in the head and I felt so bad, I turned around and grabbed him by the neck and I was mad. I was crying and mad and got to choking him. I was choking him, the more I choked, the longer his neck got. Well they were laughing at first but then Uncle Oliver got scared because he saw the goose's neck was getting longer. I had to stop awhile and rest but the goose's head fell over on the ground and his neck was all stretched out. Uncle Oliver yelled "Quit, quit choking him!" Uncle Philip said, "No, you let that goose beat up on him coming and a going! Go on Junior and do what you want to do." I choked until I was tired. That goose finally got up and staggered around and after two or three days when I went in there that goose would hide from me. He would hide up there with all the chicks. He never did peck me on the head again.

Stool for the Fire

I was going to a one room school house for a little bit of my life and it had a couple of different classes going on in it at one time. They had a pot bellied stove in it, and my job was to start the fire early. My job was to put the coal in and empty the ashes. I took care of my stove. Well back then when you wanted to go to the bathroom you had to go to the outhouse. You had to go up and let the teacher know. The way you let her know was to hold up one finger for one thing and two fingers for the other. The boy behind me held up his hand to signal that he had to go to the outhouse. So she let him go. He came back then another ten minutes later he had to go again, so he held up his hand. Well she wouldn't let him go. He was sitting there whimpering and he got up and started towards the teacher. I was the first one to notice. There were little turds falling out of his breeches leg trailing him up to the teacher's desk. I busted out laughing. The teacher saw that he had crapped his overhauls. She told him to go out to the hydrant and clean himself up. She led him out, and when she came back in, she wore my butt out big time. She started whooping me and I told her, "Why are you whooping me, I didn't shit those turds, he did!" She liked to beat me to death. When she got done she told me to clean it up. I got my little shovel and coal bucket and went to clean up behind him. When she wasn't looking I opened the door to the stove and threw the whole load in there. Lord have mercy! That was the worst thing I could have done. Because of that school let out a little earlier than it usually did that day. She whooped me some more. I didn't know how they knew at home but by the time I got home, they started whooping me too. My butt was so damn red and so sore, that for two months if you wanted a fire lit somewhere, I could have dropped my britches, aimed at a spot, and it would have burst into flames.

Twin Prize Fighters

Years ago, grown-ups, not all, but some would do this. They would get kids together and have them challenge each other. They would say, "I bet you can't take him!" They would get you fighting and wrestling each other. You would fight like heck. That's the way my foster uncle, Oliver would do with my foster cousin Phillip and me. Phillip was two years older than me. I tried every way I could to whoop him. He was a lot stronger than me and I could never beat him. He had a little penny nose and I would hit that nose. Before I knew it he had whooped me real good. When we were in school it was different, if anybody ever picked on me, Philip would take up for me. In Lenoir City, I was in grammar school and there were these two twins. For some reason, I could take one of them, but not the other. They were identical, I couldn't tell them apart at all. I would always get into it with the one I could whoop. He would pick a fight, then, when we would meet up after school, he would change with the other twin and that twin would whoop my butt. I told Phillip about it. He said, "Well next time, you meet them out there at the big ole hickory tree. I will hide out there and when you all get ready to fight, I will step in and trade places with you." So, sure enough, I couldn't wait for that guy to pick a fight with me. So sure enough he did and we got all lined up out there by that big ole tree. I told him, "This is one time I am going to wear your ass out!" He was tickled to death. He figured it would go down the same way. Well right before I started the fight with the tougher twin, Phillip stepped out from behind that tree and said, "Hey you come here!" You could just see the look on his face. He didn't want any part of Phillip and Phillip said to me, "You stand here and you take him on (the lesser twin)". The one that was laughing got his little butt wore out and I never had any more trouble from him from that day forth!

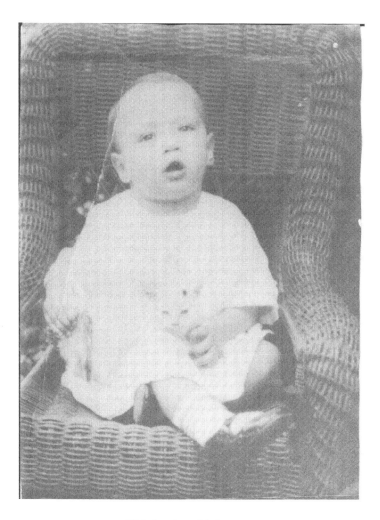

Chick, Age Unknown

Chick, Age 5

Tennessee Industrial School by Will Dodson

In order to set the stage for the next set of stories let me tell you about Tennessee Chicken's life as an orphan.

My dad had a habit of running away. He would run off and live on the streets, sleeping in automobiles, which were left unattended as well as cardboard boxes filled with newspaper for insulation. He said he felt the safest when it was dark as nobody could see him. He bathed in creeks when he slept in the woods and he found food when he could. He tells the story of making it a habit of going into a particular drug store and buying a drink on his way out. Only problem was that while he was there he would go ahead and order a meal and eat it, only paying for the drink when he went back out of the drug store. He thought he was really getting away with something, but in actuality the staff there knew he was an orphan on his own and paid for his meals out of their pockets. He would return sometime later and attempt to pay those folks back.

Dad kept running away from foster homes and kept getting back onto the streets until the Sullivan County Court decided Dad's fate and as a ward of the State he was sent to the Tennessee Industrial School in Nashville, Tennessee. This would later be called the Tennessee Preparatory School.

The following stories, told by Tennessee Chicken, take place during Dad's time at the Tennessee Industrial School.

Chick(en)

I was sent to the Tennessee Industrial School (TIS) in Nashville, TN in the 1940s. I had run away from foster families so many times that the Sullivan County Court decided to send me to TIS.

At that time, TIS was a school where a kid who didn't have but one parent or didn't belong in a reform school, could live. Sullivan County paid my way because I didn't have parents. Once there, you were put in different dormitories. I was in the ninth division. There was a lady matron and her husband, who looked over my dormitory. There were seventy kids in my dormitory. There were two different ends to the dormitory and we all had our own beds. The girl's dormitory was at one end of campus and boy's was at the other end. Each had their own kitchens and dining rooms. We ate at the big dining room that fed three or four different dormitories. They had older boys working the tables. They set the tables with the plates and cups. The food came in big aluminum bowls. They would bring all the kids in and we would stand there while they said the blessing. After that was over, you would pass the bowl.

This old boy at our table was a great big ole boy. I believe I was 11 or 12. I was young and small, but I was built. This boy was already in high school, big ole boy. He sat at the end of the table and I sat on his side. While they were saying the blessing, he spit in the bowls of food, where he could eat all he wanted. Those kids would wait and take the food. I thought, well shit, after he spit in it, I didn't want it. Everyone was scared of him. I went two or three days and I was getting hungry. Well, there was a field nearby where they had turnip greens. I was eating them raw. I got so hungry I thought I was going to die, but I didn't want that food after he spit in it. They let the kids out but the boys running the table had to stay and clean up the dishes and they were late getting out. Well, we got out and we were playing around. I saw this house sitting at one end of the campus and there was a bunch of chickens running around that evening. I told the other boys, "Shit, I'm going to have me some fried chicken tonight fellas!" I ran one of them down. I rang its neck and I skinned him. I just pulled all the hide off and took some sticks and built a fire and started cooking him and he was probably half raw but I started eating it anyway. All at once, those kids yelled, "Jigger, run!!!" I didn't know who Jigger was, but I found out. Those kids took off. This fella walked up and he had seen me and asked what I was doing. I said I was having some chicken and he said, "Don't you get enough to eat in the cafeteria." I said, "No. I can't eat that food." He said, "Where did you get the chicken?" I said, "Well I just got me one." He said, "Well, what's that on its leg?" It had a red ringer on the leg. People put those on the chicken's legs so that they knew who the chickens belonged to. Then he said, "That's funny mine have red ringers too." I started to take off and he caught me and he reached up and looked like he tore half a tree limb off. He wore my butt out. I thought he'd never quit. When he got done, he said, "Now I want you to tell me why you killed that chicken, you can't be that hungry." I said, "Yeah I am, the boy at our table is a big ole boy, while they say the blessing and you have your head bowed, he spits in the food." He paused and looked and me and asked, "Are you telling the truth? I said, "Yeah, I've eaten those old raw turnips until I thought I would die." He said, "I am George and I work the yard. You have to take care of yourself out here." I said, "Ok." "Now go on back to your dormitory", he said. I went on back and didn't tell anybody anything. That was on a Friday. On Saturday after breakfast they would usually have cheese toast and chili and it was already fixed. A buddy of mine Bill sat at my end. He told me he was going home that weekend and so he said I could have his meal. So while the blessing was being said, this big ole boy reached across me to get Bill's bowl. When he reached, I stabbed his hand and he didn't make a sound at all. I thought my God, he's tough. He looked at me and said, "I'm fixin' to kill you." I said, "Lord have mercy." I got so damn scared that my throat filled up and wanted to give him all the chili I had, I knew I was dead. I was so scared I couldn't eat, I left most of it. We went outside. Well it would be thirty or forty minutes before he got out. When you had trouble everyone would make a circle so no adults could see if there was a fight. Two or three boys said they would help me. I said no need for everyone getting hurt. There was no need to hide. The worst thing you could do was squeal as you'll hear about later, Reader. I was sitting by the door and I was scared to death, I'm not lying. I did everything but I knew this boy was going to kill me. Finally, the door opened and he came out. I don't know how close he got to me but I closed my eyes as tight as I could get them. I ran and I leapt and everything went blank and stood still. I was biting and clawing and scratching, I heard him screaming and I had bit the tip of his nose off. Blood was just flying. I was so damn scared I didn't know if he hit me or what. They had to take him to the hospital. Mr. Menzler, the "Boss", had me brought to the main office where he was. He came up there. You weren't allowed to tell anything, if you were a snitch they would gang up on you. I thought, well I'm in trouble. The "Boss" was giving me the third degree. I couldn't tell him the truth. He was telling me he didn't know what to do with me. "Guess we will have to send him to Jordonia", (which was a reform school in Tennessee). They were discussing what they were going to do with me. The boy had gone to the hospital to get worked on. While they were standing there, George, the man that whooped my ass earlier, walked in having found out about it. Mr. Menzler was about to carry me to reform school. Mr. George said, "No Boss, hold on a minute, what happened out there is my fault. What took place is my fault. This kid told me everything that went down. I should have went right then and checked it out but I took too long. This boy has been spitting in the food." They got everybody at my table and they all told the truth. Mr. Menzler still chewed me out. From that day on nobody picked on me no more. That's how I got my nickname of "Chick". Up until that time in my life everybody had called me Junior but Mr. George nicknamed me "Chicken" after the chicken I stole from him. Well later that was shortened to "Chick". So that's how I got my name folks.

Mr. Menzler

I was crazy about Mr. Menzler. He was called "the boss"; he was the superintendent at TIS. He had come here from Germany and Hitler had killed most of his family during World War II. Mr. Menzler had studied to be a preacher and he was good with kids. He was super. But the time I came out there I didn't know nothing about Germans or anything like that. He was a big man and he was strict, but he ended up being one of the nicest men I would ever know. He would later be tragically killed by the same type of kid that he spent his whole life saving. You see reader, he was in New York and he was diabetic and he would leave his door unlocked when he would have spells. Some young kids broke in to rob him and beat him. His funeral was one of the biggest I had ever seen. He was a good man. The first time I met him was in Sullivan County, when the judge and sheriff decided I would be sent to TIS. Judge said he had to go to Memphis so said he would carry me down to Nashville. We left Kingsport in a Hudson and the sheriff was driving and I had the backseat. They fed me good and gave me ice cream. They treated me real good. It was late at night when we got there and dark and everybody had gone to bed. All the dormitories were asleep. Mr. Menzler came up and he was in pajamas and a white robe and sat behind a desk in the main building. I had a little old suit coat and a Dick Tracy hat. I thought I was something. I had a pack of cigarettes that they didn't know about. When they left, the boss hadn't got there. The assistant superintendent was there and he said, "Sit down son, Mr. Menzler will be here in a minute." I sat there by myself and broke out a Lucky Strike, lit it, and started smoking. Mr. Menzler said, "What are you doing son? Hey, where did you get that cigarette? We don't smoke out here son." I said, "I don't give a damn about what you do. I smoke." He said, "Well you won't do it here." I said, "That's what you think." He reached behind a cabinet and looked like he pulled out a buggy whip and he started whooping me. Every time he hit me I said, "You ole sonofabitch." I finally shut up and I almost quit smoking. He called Mrs. Hollingsworth and they put me in the 9th Division. Even when I was older and was smoking a cigarette and I saw him coming I would throw it away as fast as I could.

Whippin's

It was about the third night I was at TIS there are long dormitories, single bunks all the way down. They holler, "lights out!" When they say that, there is no talking, no nothing. You aren't supposed to do anything. I hadn't been there long and some guy let out a hell of a fart. Hoppy Hawthorne, he could fart the Star Spangled Banner, it was God's truth, he could drag it along like a tune. I'm serious. Anyway, he let a fart and everybody got to laughing. Ole man Hollingsworth wanted to know what was going on. Nobody would tell anything. He said, "By God you are going to tell or I'll whoop your butts!" He was going to give everybody three licks. So he whooped two butts and got to mine. I said, "I'm not taking a whooping. He started it, he farted!" I pointed to the kid that started the whole thing.

Mr. Hollingsworth whooped his butt. Nobody said anything.

A couple of days passed by and we were in the cow lot. There was a big baby buggy down there. All of a sudden, the boys tied me in that and took one of those young calves and tied its tail to the buggy and kicked it in the ass and the calf took off. That calf drug me everywhere. I was upside down and everywhere in between. The calf then ran between two bushes and broke lose. I felt like I was half dead. They let me know right then and there that you don't squeal on anybody. That's when I learned not to tell. When I was asked later about my bruises I said I fell off a barn I had climbed. Speaking of butt whooping, a common theme to my life. My agriculture teacher would whip you and he was built like a bull. He would make you get on the corner of the table for your whopping. He would get you for anything and give you three licks. That sonofabitch had made me get on the corner of the table, that corner would catch your groin every time he hit you. Well way later, I was in High School. I was walking along with Billie Joe when I saw that same teacher bent over at the water fountain. He was bent over taking a drink and I saw his big ole fat ass sticking out there. Billie Joe knew what I had to do. Near there was a closet with brooms and janitorial stuff. I opened the door and got a heavy broom. I snuck down there and I reared back and hit that sonofabitch as hard as I could hit him and he butted his head. It skinned his head and knocked two of his teeth out. He fell out in the floor. I just put the broom back and walked on. Everybody hated him and left him laying there. Nobody said a word.

Another similar story, Webb was the cook. Me and Bill P. and a bunch of us were in the kitchen. There were these big ole steam pots, they cooked the meals in. I had white rice in mine. Bill had turnip greens in his. Mr. Webb told Bill P. to open up the six cans of turnip greens and put them in the pot with rice in it. Bill tried to object but Mr. Webb said, "Don't but me, put six gallons in there." Bill was going to tell him it was rice. So he opened the six cans and dumped them in. I just stirred the rice and turnip greens. When he found out that the rice had turnip greens it didn't go over too good. He made us take it all to the hog pen. It was a long way from the kitchen to the hog pen. He made us carry those turnip greens up there and it took us a long time and he wouldn't let us carry little buckets, about a gallon a piece or so. We didn't even get to eat supper until we got it up to the hog pen. He also always whooped our butts. He had a big ole paddle with holes in it where the air would go through and provide a better butt whooping. Anyways, we had to spend all that time carrying all that crap up to the hog pens. There was Billie Joe, Ralph and me. You had three of us to fight if you messed with one. Anyway, that was while we were younger. It was summertime and Mr. Webb had screen doors on the kitchen so the heat would go out. He really knew how to work those ovens. He made good cakes, bread, and anything you wanted. Well we were walking along and those steam pots had boat paddles, like a canoe paddle. They had those hanging by the pots which were close to the stove. He was in there and looking at his cornbread and the oven was hot. It hit me again. Mr. Webb was bent over looking at that cornbread. I looked at Billie Joe and he read my mind, he held the screen door open and I grabbed a paddle and hit his big ole ass and he went head first in the oven and it burnt the hell out of his head. I think the kids pulled him out of there. They never told who it was. They wouldn't tell on you back then.

Jumpin' in the Honeypot

As I mentioned earlier, when I was at TIS in the 1940s I had a friend named Billy Joe. His nickname was 8 Ball. He had a brother named Ralph and another one named Lloyd. We ran together. Billy Joe and Ralph and Lloyd's mother was from Memphis. She would come and pick them up at TIS. Since I didn't have anybody, Billy Joe asked if I could go with them. She said it was fine and so I went with them to Memphis. It was on the weekend and around a holiday. I believe it was around the Fourth of July. Billy Joe had an older brother and he had an old car with a big two seater trunk in the back. Well we left and went over to West Memphis, in Arkansas, and there were some old joints over there. Some of them had some moonshine-like drinks, tasted that way anyway. We were sneaking in and out of places. We came out, and I was walking down the road, and as far as you could see down the road, were fireworks, which people had set out. I never saw so many in my life! Back in those days, the majority of the time, people carried matches for their cigarettes. (I had those old nickel matches that came out of those old nickel box matches.)Well, I decided to smoke a cigarette. I struck a match on the side of my leg, lifted the match to my cigarette and threw the match. Boy, I'm tellin' you, the sky lit up and there were fireworks going off all over the place. I had caught one on fire, which shot out into others that were lying around and before I knew it, the entire place was set off in fireworks. The sky was all lit up and smoke was just bellowing out. You never saw the chaos! Well somebody saw me do it and he let out a yell. I took off running through the nearby cornfield as fast as my feet could carry me. Before I had hit the edge of the cornfield, the same man that yelled had drawn a pistol. Hell, they were all hunting for me, wanting to kill me. I was running down that cornfield and I didn't know what to do. I think that they were gypsies or something. They sounded like it, smelled like it. But one thing was for sure, and that was that they were mad, and they were chasing me like hell. I kept on running, and I saw this place by the highway. It was an old Gulf filling station and I ran up to it. There was a big ole truck there and there was a door open in the cab. So I thought, well I will hide in this cab, they won't find me here. Then I got to thinking, no if they come through here, they are going to see me hiding up in this thing. So I got out and I thought to myself, where the hell can I hide and still watch the road and see if Billy Joe and his brothers were nearby. Well, all of a sudden a mob of these gypsies could be heard coming nearby. I looked up and there was a lid open on the tank of the truck. So I climbed up and drop down into it. I didn't have time to run for the cornfield again, they would have seen me! It seemed like they all had guns. The tanker truck had a little ladder in it and I went flying down the ladder and got down in it and shut the lid. There was some stuff in it and by stuff, I don't mean oil. I had dropped in a tank of pure 100% shit. I had it almost up to my knees and I closed that lid. I could hear the gypsies moving in on the area and cursing and saying that I was probably hiding out in that cornfield somewhere. Well, they left and I came out of that tank and got out on that road and lay down in the ditch. Soon Billy Joe and his brother came by in their car and I stunk so bad they wouldn't let me in the car. They put me in the trunk and you have never heard people complain so much. The smell that was coming off of me was radiating through the car out of the trunk and boy it would kill you. I'm not kidding you. But, I was safe and crappy, or happy.

The Boxing Match

At TIS at that time we had one of the best boxing teams in the country, we had a boxing coach named "Larky". He had been a pro fighter from Nashville. He had won a lot of championships boxing and he was so good that he fought the guy that fought Joe Lewis. He was a light heavy weight. His manager tried to push him ahead, the guy he lost to fought Joe Lewis later on. He finally didn't advance like he could have. He was ready for heavy weight. He ended up at TIS, he was our barber and boxing coach and turned out some of the best boxers Tennessee had ever had. The only haircut he could give that was worth a crap was a GI. He would just shave you bald headed. So he must have made more money boxing.

They would have boxing matches. There would be kids from other places come there. A lot of times they would fight at the Hippodrome, golden gloves and fights where you paid to get in. We had them at our gym. They would have a ring out there. If you were small and little they would put those big ole gloves on you, bigger than your head. I thought I would try to box. Well I wasn't too thrifty on my feet, always clumsy, bowlegged, knees weak. I staggered around. I decided I would be a boxer. I did pretty good a fight or two. They brought a group in there. Larky would go up and grab those ropes and put his foot on his bottom foot and hold them and let you go in, he would then jump the ropes. I thought if he can do that I can to. I decided I would leap in. Well I leaped and that was the last thing I remember. When I came to, they had taken me back there on a board. I opened my eyes and come to and Larky was standing there. I asked, "How'd I do?" He said, "You done pretty good Chick, you almost got in the ring."

I tried another fight and got hit at the end of the chin, I wasn't a fighter, and I had a jaw of precious glass.

The Devil's Gonna Getcha

Reader, there's no doubt that I could get in more shit than anybody. One day with a little time on our hands, some boys and me at the Tennessee Industrial School decided we thought it might be a good idea to sniff some ether. We got a couple cans of it and went out on the football field. Well like everything else I took too big a breath in and it knocked me out. I was laying there in a nightmare. The devil was reaching up through that football field and got his hands on me. I was screaming and fighting. Ain't no way I was gonna let him take me. He pulled and I fought back and this seemed to go on forever. Well I finally broke free when I woke up. I swore to myself right then and there I was never going to do that again and I was so scared that the devil was gonna get me that I promised that I wouldn't fight, cuss, steal, drink, smoke or do anything like that for a couple years.

Korea by Will Dodson

Dad was in the National Guard in his later years out at TIS. He had tried to enlist when World War II broke out but he was way too young and the recruiters laughed and told him to come back in a few years. Dad left TIS and enlisted in the Navy right before the Korean War escalated. He jumped a train leaving Union Station in Nashville, Tennessee and headed out to California for training. The following stories take place in the 1950s during the height of the Korean conflict and are a few stories he has told from that period. Many stories he has held back due to terrors he witnessed over there and the conditions he survived. He would later be on the ground and would experience frost bite and be a part of conflicts, which would haunt him for several decades.

David's & Goliath

We were in Hollywood, California. We had been on liberty and there was Billy Joe, me, and Willie V. We had joined the same time and we were in boot camp together. Well, we had been up to Hollywood to see some of the shows and different stage shows. We saw Dean Martin and went to a few movies and things. We went to a couple of dances and they wouldn't serve us drinks because we were considered minors even though we were in the service. The women that could legally drink wouldn't mess with us because they had to buy our drinks for us. It was hard for us to have fun or get any dates. I ain't never been for that, I think if you put that uniform on you ought to be able to go buy a drink anywhere in the world, in fact, you ought to get the first two or three free! We were half way mad about it and we weren't really completely out of boot camp at that time. Anyway, we got some wino to go buy us a jug. We sneaked in the alley and we all got to drink that stuff, just like down South, you can go in one of those joints and after you have a few drinks you grow ten feet tall and bullet proof. We stood there and drank that and talked about how bad it was that the US wouldn't let servicemen buy drinks. So we got big and bad, we were in the service and had just gotten out of boot camp and we were about to go to Korea and whoop everybody! The more we drank, the taller we got and it was a surprise we could even get through the door of a bar with as big as we had grown. We walked around looking in windows. We came to this one bar and it had those swinging doors like you have seen in cowboy movies. We looked in and there were two or three tables and a few people. Behind the bar I saw one waitress standing at the customer side and behind the bar there was an old man stacking bottles. I said,

"There is nobody in here, let's go get drinks". I don't think it was me, but it could have been. I was loudmouthed then just like I am now. One of us said, "By God we are minors, we are here to stay and we are having a drink!" We walked in and I ain't kidding you. This is the truth! The biggest man I ever seen in my life came up from under that bar. He was the biggest man I ever laid eyes on. At that time I weighed 140 pounds soaking wet with my clothes on. Billy Joe weighed 150 at the most. Willie V. was a great boxer and he weighed a full 112 pounds. This guy straightened up and walked over. I froze in my tracks. I am telling you, I wouldn't lie; the thought of fighting that man was the furthest thing that ever come in my mind. I looked and I froze and I couldn't believe it. The man was real nice; he didn't get mad or threaten us or nothing. He said, "Gentlemen, I am sorry, there is no serving minors." He walked over and he grabbed us by the nap of the neck. Willie's head came up to the guy's belt and Willie started boxing. There he was holding me and Billy Joe and there was Willie punching on him with all he had. He picked us up just as nice as you please and our feet weren't even touching the ground. Thank God he threw Billy Joe first so I had somebody to land on. Billy Joe went past the sidewalk and into the street and I was on top of him. I looked back and Willie was still whooping on him and the guy was laughing and he just reached down and grabbed Willie on top of his head and picked him up, like picking up an orange, and grabbed him by the seat of the britches, and threw him out. He stood there laughing. No time did he even get mad. We got away quick and got to laughing about Willie trying to whoop him. Later on, that man was big like Hoss Cartwright on Bonanza and I saw him on television. He was in a bar, could have been the same one and he could take beer caps, three of them and put them between his fingers and he could close his hand and bend those caps three at a time. I'm telling the truth. He was strong! He wasn't the kind of fella that you would want to try to whoop. You just salute him and go the other way!

Teeth

Nowadays you see people with pretty white, straight, and perfect teeth on television and in the movies. When I was in the service I had a tooth that was bad. My jaw was swelling up and I had to get it fixed. The dentist drilled it and fixed and then he told me. "Boy, I will tell you one thing. All of you Southern men have the worse teeth in the country. You have bad teeth and you lose them. You don't take care of them!" I said, "What do you mean we don't take care of them?" He said "Well, you don't take care of them. You don't brush them and take care of your gums." I said "I didn't see much use in brushing teeth anyways. The only reason you brush your teeth is after you eat something. When you don't eat but every other day or so, you don't really have a need to brush them!" That's the truth, he had to laugh.

Back when mom would carry me to Washington D.C. I noticed that kids in school in the big city would eat good. I was up there and they gave us little bottles of milk and graham crackers. They took care of us and fed us good. The number one thing I ate in Washington was chili. I ate more chili and watermelon up there. Down here in Tennessee when I went to grammar school, the only thing they gave us free was Pepsodent tooth paste and a tooth brush. I didn't have to brush my teeth two or three times a day because all we had back then was yellow grits and as far as I know they don't hurt teeth!

Navy Nopants

Coming back from overseas I don't remember which destroyer it was. USS Fisk, USS Kennedy, one of the two. I made two around the world trips on it and we were coming back into New York. Well the Statue of Liberty is really in New Jersey. When you come in like that, you have to go top side. You line up on both sides of the ship standing at parade dress or attention. Sometimes the ship gives salute. People cheer you in. You've been trained that if you fall in the water you are supposed to swim away from the ship fast because the undertow can get you. They have gun shields and I was at the 40 mm gun shield. They are for anti-aircraft for enemy planes. They have sides to them with latches and you drop that side and throw all your hulls into the water in combat. You save them in practice. Anyway the sides are supposed to be locked at all times unless you walk them to unload the brass. I got lazy and leaned back against the side and when I leaned back I went plum over the side in the damn water. It was cold weather too. We are trained if you hit the water, you take your breeches off and blow them up and make a life jacket out of it. Well all the training I got went to hell. When I took my breeches off, I took my drawers and breeches off and everything, I lost every damn thing. Usually they drop one of those whale boats next to the ship. This time they had choppers nearby. One came by and pulled me up out of that cold water and I was butt naked. Of course they had a picture. You talk about shrinkage, instead of being a sailor I could have been a woman. It was all drawn up. I didn't think I would ever get it all workin' again.

Wheelin' and Dealin' in Italy

There's nobody more crooked than Italians, in my opinion. I've known some good ones in my time and I've known some good ones that are thieves. I was over there, when I was in the Navy, and they sold me a big basket full of rolls with meat hanging out of them. The minute the vendor sold it to me, he took off running and they had taken a razor blade and had made little cuts on the rolls, there was no meat. I got to throwing those rolls at him and if I had hit him with one it would have knocked his brains out.

Well this one time the Captain's gig had to be put in the water and we were going to run it a little bit to check it. We were close to the dock. While I had it down I ran it a little bit. There were a bunch of damn Italians so I sold it to them. I took the money for it and they took off. Well the minute they took off they got caught and I went aboard the ship. They caught them and they said someone sold it to them. They called everybody aboard to find out who did it. The chief asked me if I did it or not. "Hey you know anything about this?" he said. I told him the truth. He said, "I don't think you should be present. We don't want this to get out." They called quarters for everybody. Everyone lined up and one guy answered for me and I wasn't there. They didn't find me because I didn't go to roll call.

Taking Another Dip in the Honeypot

Mommasan in Japanese is the head woman of the house. She ran the business in the out of bound places, which would be a cat house of sorts. Well, we were getting ready to go on liberty. When you go on liberty you go up on the ship and there is a bulletin board that tells you where not to go because shore patrol or MPs will get you, it's out of bounds. But those are the best places to go because they are cheaper. So I forget if we were in Yokohama or Sassabo or Youkuska, one of those places. I was in this out of bound place where I wasn't supposed to be and in Japan the Occupation was still on at that time. Things were not that good in Japan until later on after the Korean War. I was in this out of bounds place and I shouldn't have been in it, it was a Japanese cathouse. Mommasan yelled for the MPs. So there was a window there and while she was hollering I ran in the window and jumped out and when I did I jumped in a "honey pot". A honey pot is a barrel they kept outside where they kept all the human waste. They used it on their gardens for fertilizer. It was deep and there I was. I had a white uniform on waist deep. It stunk, lord have mercy. I just stood there and I couldn't run around town like that. A big ole MP looked out and we were nose to nose, neither of us said anything. The captain inside asked if anybody was outside. He said, "No sir, there's nobody here!" They didn't want to carry me back like that. I was raising hell when they left. Mommasan got me back in there and she put me in a big ole tub of hot water with a fire underneath it. By the time they got me clean she almost had my uniform clean. How she did it, I will never know. I got a lot of good services out of jumping in that barrel. They didn't want me to be unpleased. They were very nice to me. I looked like a new penny when I left out there. You don't ever forget that smell, whew! I can still smell it today!

I was in Yokuska, Japan. Anyway, I had been somewhere and with the occupation still on you had to be back to the ship by midnight. That was curfew. We were anchored out and had a tender to bring us in and out. I come in and when I walked into the tender dock a helluva fight had broken out. This frog man was fighting and he thought I stood up to fight and I was in line to be next. He told me, "I will be with you directly." So, I sucker-punched him and he just shook his head and said again, "I'll get to you later!" So hell, I took off running and went around the corner and I was moving and he was after me and all of a sudden I fell into a lake of shit. He couldn't outrun me. I had those flat feet going. I ran into one of those reservoirs. I was treading shit and when he saw me he said, "Forget it, I don't want you now!" Funny thing is he did throw me a lifesaver. I had to get back on the ship. If you missed that tender you were in trouble. I stunk to high hell and I almost threw up myself. I was in the front of the tender and I stunk so damn bad, but they crank up in the front and that air coming off me hit all of them. They said, "My God, what in the hell is that smell!" Finally, there was an officer and they pointed at me. "Throw him over!" they said. It was a mile and a half 'til my ship. The officer said no. They put me on the deck of the ship and they took one of those water hoses and washed my ass off. I had to throw my whites away, they were ruined. I was the honey pot kid.

Ella Fitzgerald

I was in New York. Everyone wanted to see Times Square. During the day I saw Tony Bennett. We went to see a movie and a stage show. They had step brothers, black dancers, they were really good. All the girls were fainting and passing out. I didn't know who he was. He sang "forever be a beggar" and later that night we were at the Silver Dollar in Manhattan and it was a beer joint. They had a good deal on beer and women. Somebody saw where Ella Fitzgerald was playing at Bird Land. It was a black nightclub and you had to be dressed up formal to be there. Of course, we were half drunk. We decided we'd go. Well when we got up there, the man at the door didn't want to let us in. The uniform should cover you as dress, but I guess he thought we were too drunk. We were arguing that we were on our way to Korea to die and he wouldn't let us in and we couldn't believe it. I said they wouldn't stop me. There was a fella came to the door and he was as big as three double doors. He said, "Bring them on in!" There was me, Tony, and Green. They sat us right by the stage and he gave us a round of drinks. Ella Fitzgerald came on and she put on one hell of a show. She could act like Louie Armstrong and imitate him. She came and sat at our table and she was the sweetest thing. I was so proud. I had her autograph. I also had Dean Martin's autograph at the Carnation in California. I had a lot of that; I was good at getting those autographs. I wasn't ashamed to get them. I never did get Bob Hope's but I wanted it.

Driving Nails In My Coffin

I'm just telling stuff as it comes to my mind, I remember when I was over in Japan. I told you that I loved music but I didn't listen to country music much. We were in Japan and it was dark and we were walking down the street. We had been in a few of those joints that just consisted of boards lying over barrels. I had drunk too much of the Japanese beer and I was walking around and one of those Japs had one of those big record players in one of those places and he had it cranked up. It was Ernest Tubbs singing "I'm Just Driving Nails In My Coffin" and I couldn't stand Ernest Tubbs back then and I got to thinking about Ernest Tubbs and the Grand Ole Opry and 5th Avenue and Church Street, the Krystal on the corner and the orange bar nearby it. All of a sudden I got homesick. There is nothing that hurts worse than that. Well I got to crying and carrying on. Well Green and them thought that somebody had stabbed me. There were still some Japanese at the time, who didn't care for Americans being right after the end of the war and all. Well they found out I was just homesick. If I could have, I would have swam all the way back to Nashville. I thought about that for years afterwards because I could never stand Ernest Tubbs or Roy Acuff, but I loved them that night!

Fats and Fights

Fats Domino put on a helluva show for all the servicemen. Marines, Army, everybody was there. We were in this big ole building and he was really putting on a show. They had a pitcher of beer for cheap. We were sitting there drinking. He was putting on a show and singing when a fight broke out. Sometimes servicemen get to fighting. The Navy, Marines, Army all thinks they are the toughest. When a fight breaks out the best thing to do is to hide under the table. Fats never missed a beat, just kept playing. I sat under the table with a pitcher of beer and beer flying everywhere and I just kept drinking until it was over with. He was singing "Blueberry Hill".

Whiskey from a Water Fountain

I believe it was the USS Fisk. Anyway, they had a boy on there; they called him "Frenchie". He was Cajun from Louisiana from Via Platz, or something like that. Well he was an engineer and he worked in the engine room and had tattoos all over him. He was bald headed and had a spider web on his head. Going around his body he had hound dogs chasing a rabbit and butt naked there was half a rabbit going up his butt with a hound right after it. He had been in the Navy quite awhile. He had the water cooler rigged, where he could switch it and get something to drink. He made peach brandy and raisin jack. It was good. I don't know how he got away with it. He could switch a lever and get water or get that booze out of the fountain. You would take a cup down there and fill it up and let him know and he would fix it where you could fill up. I had a canteen cup, you had to pay him, but it was good stuff.

Tallywacker

I'm telling you, this is something else. There could be a movie made about being circumcised after you're 20 years old. That's a movie in itself. Back when I was born nobody went to a doctor. I was delivered by a midwife. Anyway, I wasn't circumcised. Well when you get in the service, they frown on it. Most of the doctors were Jewish anyways. I didn't get circumcised. I had been around the world once. I was in Japan. The Jewish doc said I needed to be circumcised. That's all they had in that ward was circumcisions. This male nurse did not want to fool with you more than they had to. They put fear in us saying that infections could set in from dirtiness. So that scares the hell out of you. They tell you that when you get this done, to break and smell this capsule to lower your blood pressure. A hard on will bust the stitches and they have to do it all again. Whatever you do, keep your mind clean so you don't get a hard on. You get one anyway. Your buddies come see you and the first thing they bring you is a pin up magazine. I read the bible and you do everything, you can get saved getting circumcised. That's the only time in a man's life when he doesn't want to get a hard on. Anyway, I was worried to death, nobody touched mine. I took care of it myself. They got me ready, he did the job. When they do it and you wake up the next day, this S.O.B. will never be the same, it looks like a double barrel shotgun over and under, it's black and blue and looks like everything but a pecker, swelled up and looks awful, burns like fire, hurts like hell. You read the bible and do everything to keep it soft. They bring these ice packs but that doesn't help. They had these things to break and smell to lower your blood pressure or whatever it takes to keep it from getting hard. I was laying there and I was trying to get my mind blank. I went to sleep. If I ever told the truth, this is it. I was laying there and I saw a beautiful blonde, I thought where did she come from? She was gorgeous. We were going to make love, she opened up her legs and I got ready and all at once that blonde turned into a tiger and the teeth bit down on my tallywacker and all at once I woke up and my stitches were busted and I was bleeding like hell. I thought I was ruined and I would never be right again. That's hell to get circumcised after you're grown. That's why it should take place when you are a baby. Anybody against it hasn't went through it late in life.

When they put the bandage on it, looks like you have a big hunk of ham. You would have thought I was handling a newborn baby. You make sure it's washed and it's clean. I could have read the bible through nine times. I never prayed so much. Hell, I didn't pray as much in the Korean War as I did getting circumcised.

Singapore

Sometimes depending on the harbor you have to anchor out and take a fleet boat in. There were two or three ships in this harbor. One was English and two were American. We were on a destroyer in the harbor. Well, we were in a fancy hotel and we were going to leave later that night. We were drinking bottles of Champagne and we were buying it cheap. Well, all of a sudden all Hell broke loose. I never found out what happened or who did it or what, but I believe somebody undid a cork and it flew over and hit a dignitary from Singapore. Well we were told to get back to the ship. We started heading back and the MPs and the SPs were getting us out of there. Well the English were in charge and they were in control of the area. We were waiting on the fleet landing boat to go back. All at once a mob came and they were mad. One of them had a pitchfork. Where he got it, I don't know. I didn't see any hay. Well he was threatening to stab some servicemen there. An Englishman was standing there and didn't have a uniform or any military outfit but he jumped in between the chaos. He kept telling everybody to back up and they were acting like they were going to come on anyway. Well he came out with a handgun and he put it to the guy with the pitchfork's head and pulled the trigger. He dropped him right there in the street. Brains and blood splattered over the mob behind him. People started to back up and it wasn't long before English troops got there and they got the whole crowd back. We went back to the ship and I'm not sure whatever happened after that.

Viva La Castro

I was very lucky when it came to traveling. I got to go around the world twice while I was in the service. I got to go through both the Panama and Suez Canals. I went to Italy, France, Singapore, Japan and Korea. I went to Cuba, Gitmo. In fact I have a good story about Cuba…

This was after I came home from the War. I told people about being in Cuba. So one summer I went down to Daytona Beach Florida. From Daytona Beach I decided to go down to Miami. While I was in Miami I ran into Dr. D's wife Elizabeth. Her and Aunt Ethel, who worked for the State Employment Office, were going on a boat to Cuba. She asked me if I had been there before. I said yeah. She said, "Why don't you come with us and I will pay for everything." I said, "Sure, can't beat that!" So we took the boat over. We went into one of the joints known as Sloppy Joe's, known for good rum. They have a distillery that you give a dollar and a quarter and you can sample every type of rum that they make. They had anything you wanted. We got in Sloppy Joe's and had some drinks and enjoyed Cuba and as we walked out the door, somebody had written VIVA LA CASTRO! At that time Batista was in charge and Castro was in the mountains as a guerrilla trying to assume power. Well I was drunk and without thinking I shouted out "VIVA LA CASTRO!" I hadn't gotten it out of my mouth and all of a sudden a soldier with a rifle and a bayonet that looked 40 feet long had pinned me to the wall and Elizabeth and Aunt Ethel liked to have crapped in their britches and me too! I sobered up fast, believe me. They were going to arrest me and Elizabeth started arguing with them. She told them that we had just come over from Miami and I said, "I was just reading what was written on the wall. I don't know anything about Castro. Lord, we just came over." They told us, "I tell you what, the best thing that you can do is get back to the United States fast." Elizabeth figured instead of waiting for that boat tomorrow that we would just fly out that night and there were a bunch of people trying to get out of there. She bought us three tickets and that plane got up in the air and Elizabeth was raising Cain with me about carrying on like that. Well, about that time the pilot said that he was turning the plane back around and I liked to have had a heart attack and I said, "Lord have mercy, they think I am a guerilla!" We landed and they took two or three people off and they let us go and we got back and I said the Hell with Castro and Cuba too. Later on when I had to get a hernia operation Doc had not finished his internship. He was still an intern at General Hospital. He had to get Dr. P. to stand by. Dr. P. had graduated with Castro from Havana, Cuba. They were in the same college together. He said he couldn't understand how Castro had turned so mean. What happened was the US had tried to have him killed multiple times. I don't know if that is true or not.

Air Conditioning

The train used to come down the tracks with a load of coal from those mines and we used to get thrown up on the train as it would pass by. Well, we would throw pieces of coal off of the train down to the ground and people would pick it up and use it to heat their homes. I know the mines knew about it. They let us get away with it anyway. We had a house with no water on the inside. You had to tote the water in. The rent was $5 a month for a seven room house. I believe we were in Lenoir City at the time. There would be a few holes here and there and you would have to fill the holes with paper to keep the cold out. We didn't worry about the heat, we didn't have air conditioners. The first air-conditioner I ever saw was when I got back from Korea. This guy said, "Well you ought to see this air conditioner we have!" That was the very first one I ever saw. We got to looking around and a sailor had hid a beer up there and I imagine he was missing it when he came back. I'm not sure who took it. Well, Joe George was a boy I went to school with and we had a room we were renting from Mrs. King off of 25th close to Centennial Park. I went out to Pilk's Furniture on Charlotte and was looking around and they had an air conditioner and it was a hot summer. I didn't know anything about air conditioners, just knew I wanted one. It was a ton unit and I bought it. It was a big ole unit. I told Mrs. King what I was doing and she let me put it in. We installed and fired it up and hell I didn't think. I've got to overdo everything. I had it on high speed. I got to sleeping under blankets and I got to hurting. I thought I was going to die, boy. My knees, back and everything were hurting. I went out to Dr. P's on Charlotte and I said, something is wrong with me, I'm about to die. He got to check me and he asked me what I was eating and a bunch of questions and he found out I had an air-conditioner. He asked if I was sleeping under it. Well I was. We put it in another window of the house and it was strong enough to cool the whole house. So I've never been too bright.

The Hunt

There was three or four of us and we decided we would go deer hunting but back then when you bought your license in East Tennessee, you got deer, bear, boar and hog and turkey at the same time. Anyway, we went up there and carried a camper with us. We were staying down next to the road with the camper and a spot made for campers and we would hike up the side of the mountain. I was in the middle and anything that came in my area was mine. I had a .380 Winchester rifle. The day before that we were up there and we got to talking about bears and boars. I got thirsty and went up the hill and reached down and got a drink of water and was talking about how clear and clean the water was. I bet we didn't go 20 feet up the water and there was a bunch of bear and hog shit up the river. They got to bugging me. I am snake-bit when it comes to that. We went down and ate that day and decided to go hunt some more. I was busy shooting the shit and wasn't looking where I was going. Those wild hogs were crossed Arkansas razorback with a hog from Russia. Great big ole tusks. We were walking up the hill and I was ahead and had my gun off to the side carrying. There was a ledge and I reached for the ledge and grabbed a bush, when I swung up, just a little way off was the biggest hog you've ever seen. I hollered and I got my finger on the trigger and the hog headed my way. My friend shot over my shoulder right by my ear and hit that hog right between the eyes and when that hog got done sliding we were nose to nose and I shit in my breeches. I had to wash them out before I came home. Anyway, he shot that hog and I was so goddamn scared that I was afraid I was going to shoot someone because I was afraid of everything. I told them I have to go on home. It's 12 miles in between before you hit the next station. I said I would hitchhike. They carried me to Maryville and I caught the Greyhound home. The hog weighed 230 pounds.

Bootleggin'

Liquor making has been a historic art in Tennessee. I was more involved in the logistics of home-made and professional libations. I did a little hauling of spirits. Well, there was a fella in Nashville that would give you $300 to haul a load and he would tell you where to take it. Well I made a couple of runs. He had some Fords and some Mercury's that were fixed up to make runs, but I said fooey on that. I would do anything to make a dollar because times were tough and I wasn't making much money. A man could rent a red x trailer to hook behind a car, truck, or whatever. We rented a trailer and loaded it up and put some old furniture on there and we would have it look like we were moving. I had this girl I knew, a big ole fat girl and she had two young'uns. Me, her and these two young'uns would get in this truck and we were a pitiful sight. Those young'uns were as ugly as I was back then. She wasn't a beauty either. We would pass all kinds of cops and stop to eat. The cops would just look at us and laugh. She would breast feed those kids as well and a towel didn't cover everything she had. Nobody thought anything was going on. I would give her a hundred dollars out of the deal. It was a good trip. Fooling with booze on the weekend was a good way to make money. I also knew this fella, who owned a liquor store. He had a van and he would load it full of whiskey and on Sunday people could call him and I would call back and I had the van and I would make deliveries. I would call back and he would give me the address where to go and which liquor to bring. Well you couldn't get liquor on Sunday, so I would haul it. Well, one time this City Cop got to wondering what I was doing. I must have looked shady. I still had a case of whiskey in there and he got caught in traffic and I went flying by. Now I am not going to name the Church. I drove in front of this Church and I ran in there and stuck it in the Confessional Booth. Well I came back and the cop finally caught up with me. He searched the van and didn't find anything. So I went back into that church and this is the God's truth, if I ever told it. I was going to get my case of whiskey that I stuck in there. I hadn't seen anybody in there. There was a big note in the confessional booth that said "Thank You". So maybe a guardian angel got it! There has never been a dull moment in my life.

Underground Nashville

You have Printer's Alley and the Arcade Alley. There was a place called Doc's and across the street called the Ratskeller. It was a beer joint too. Well there was me and Joe George. He was one of the boys that was in my dormitory at TIS and when he was 14 he had a beard and looked like he was 25! Well anyway, he looked old and would buy beer for all of us. He was going with this girl at the time and she was a bartender down there and had control of the Ratskeller. She would close up at 12:30 or 1 AM. When they would close we would stay in there and drink until we were ready to leave. You could go back in the back and there were booths back there. The walls were nice stone walls and it looked like it was poured, it was perfect. There was a door with a big ole lock on it. We had been going down there quite a while. One night we asked her what's behind that door. She said, "I don't know." The guy that owned the place was in Atlanta at the time. Joe said, "We ought to knock that lock off and I can replace it." We cut that lock and we waited. By the time we cut it off it was late at night. We opened that thing and when we did it was an 8 ft wide and so high and they tried to tell me it was a drain system. The walls were made perfect and they ran the full distance. We could hear people in the stores up town and it went all the way up to the Federal Reserve, when we got where the Federal Reserve was, there was a steel gate and concrete poured. We got up where the capitol was and it was filled with concrete. The only thing we could figure it was built for escape for some reason. It wasn't a drain. It might have run some water, but it wasn't made for a drain. One place we found some shackles and chains. Another route went down to the river. They had a penitentiary for the army there at one point during the

Civil War. I haven't figured out to this day what that was. The whole City of Nashville has rock from Ireland under it and I still have some of it from a job I had down there.

Andy

When I was in the service I had a friend named Andy. We usually had three or four people we were close with. We used to run in groups. Andy was from West Tennessee and I was from East Tennessee. I never had met his family, of course, I didn't have any family, I was raised in a State orphanage. Andy invited me to meet the rest of his family. Before I got out of the service, Andy and I had went out to West Tennessee to Andy's family farm. The farm was about 800 acres. His daddy had been a moonshiner years ago and he was a big ole strapping country fella. He was a farmer and farmers can do it all. They are overall great handymen. He got religion at some point and he and his wife were Church of God. I told him I was getting out of the service before Andy and he said, "Well if you do come on down and stay awhile." That sounded pretty good to me because when you first get out of the service you feel like an orphan and don't know which way to turn. For awhile you are messed up. I went down there after I got out and I learned a whole lot from that man. He taught me all kinds of things. I tried to pick cotton and I tried to do it one handed. His kids would come in after school and pick more cotton in a couple hours than I did all day. Picking cotton is a hard job. I'm telling you, brother. You can't jump in there and pick a hundred pounds real quick dragging that sack along. I didn't pick it clean. One of the things I remember about Andy's dad was that he raised hogs. He also had cows, mules, and everything. He plowed with a tractor but still had mules to work. Well, we were in the barn one day. Like I said, he was a man and a half in size and had hands like five gallon buckets when he made a fist. He had a mule that was mean. The mule got him in the barn and cornered him and tried to push him up against the wall. He hit that mule with his fist right between the eyes and if that mule didn't go down to his knees, there ain't a cow in Georgia! He also had a lot of hogs. There was a fella that lived over three or farms down and had bought a new boar. That thing looked like a boar out of the East Tennessee mountains, it had tusks and was big and mean looking. He went and backed up his truck. I was scared to get out of the truck and he said, come on and look at this pretty thing! He dropped the tailgate on that truck and that hog whooped out of that truck and went through that gate and it was lucky that gate wasn't locked because he would have taken gate and all. He done serviced that female hog before we could get out of that truck good and was looking for another one. He said, "What about that!" I said, "Dang! He didn't even tip his hat and say hello or nothing, he just done the job!"

His boy, Andy was really something. I had a good time with him. We had a barber on the ship and he was real good at cutting hair, but something happened and he had to leave. The captain was running around hollering and worried about how we were going to get haircuts. I asked Andy, wasn't your Daddy a barber? He said, yeah he used to cut everybody's hair in the neighborhood. Well if your Daddy did it then it runs in the family. He agreed and told the Captain he thought he could do it. The boy had left his clippers, straight razors and all. Well the Captain said the best way to start is with me. I thought, oh Lord, he's going to get a Mohawk! Sandy did a great job; he was one of those boys that could do anything. He reminds me now of my wife. You could bet her she couldn't do something and she would do it just to show you. There was nothing she couldn't do either. Anyway, he got to cutting everybody's hair and they were coming from everywhere to get their hair cut. When he got out he opened up a barbershop with his brother and it was a fancy one. You made an appointment and they would serve you a drink. You could get a highball or something good to eat. Of course you paid for it but he had a world of customers.

I remember another story from that family. Andy's daddy and oldest brother lived on two pieces of land that joined together. Marvin was his oldest brother and he had a bunch of old coon hounds. He had one named Sam. He loved that ole coon hound. They would go sit out at night with those coons howling. Me and Andy would drive a tractor down those old country roads and we would carry a shotgun with us. One would drive awhile and the other would straddle the front of the tractor and we would go rabbit hunting. Rabbits would run across the road at night. We would get a bunch of rabbits to carry back and cook. We were going by Marvin's place and I was on the tractor with my legs dangling down. When Sam came running out he ran over and bit my leg dangling down. He bit me good too. He tore my britches leg up. I was sitting there with a shotgun but there was no way I could shoot him because Marvin loved that dog and if I shot him, they would have shot me. Just because a dog's tail is wagging don't mean that he won't bite you because they sure will!

Route 66

Me and Harold were hanging out one fine evening. I met Harold in a printing shop we worked at over on Pearl Street. We got drunk one Saturday and decided we were going to California and make some real money. We were making about 75 cents an hour, which was the going price for working in Nashville. We were both renting a room and paying $15 a week for room and board. We had heard about the gold rush and more money to be made. We got out a map and decided we would go Route 66. We started hitchhiking on the highway and we had old suitcases with our duds. Harold had got a hold of one of those big UT "T"s and he put it on his suitcase. Well we got picked up and were hitching rides pretty good for awhile, but when we were going through Oklahoma City, I will never forget it. The capital in Oklahoma City looks a lot like the capitol in Nashville but it has oil rigs around it. I thought Route 66 would be a big ole 4 lane highway but at some parts it becomes a small country road. There wasn't as much traffic or business as you would think. It was summertime and things were hot and dry. When we got out there on Route 66, they didn't want to serve you any water. They would give you one glass of water and after that they would charge you for it. I was charged 10 cents or a quarter for a tray of ice and it didn't last anytime out there. We drank a lot of warm water, because you couldn't keep ice. At night in the desert you would burn up. At night you would freeze to death. It got cold as hell at night. We were out in the middle of somewhere, maybe Texas. We were on Route 66 and it got really cold. It being summer we didn't have any mackinaw coats or anything because it was summer. There wasn't any traffic on Route 66 back then. When you got within 80 miles from California, everything broke off Route 66. The last 80 to 100 miles was like Death Valley. There wasn't any main traffic. We were about to freeze to death out there and I got on one side of the highway and Harold got on the other and we were going to hitch hike back. Nothing was coming. There was some old broken down shack near the road with some old dry boards. We pulled off those boards and he had some kind of magazine he had bought and we built a fire in the middle of the road. When we lit that fire there was something in that desert. Looked like a porcupine, but not sure. A bunch of them came around drawn to the heat. I got scared. We were out there with boards and using them like golf clubs knocking those sonofabitches all over the place. I thought it would never get day light. I was scared of them and freezing too. It came close to day light and a truck of Indians came by and carried us home. We almost never made it to California. It wasn't a beautiful trip, back then it wasn't built up like it is now. It wasn't anything like the song. You go to St. Louis and Joplin

Missouri and Oklahoma City is mighty pretty! None of that crap to the best of my memory. Of course I did forget a lot of it!

Lakeside Terror

This friend of mine that I worked with came by one Sunday and he had a new car he had just bought. Didn't look like much to me. It was a little convertible. He asked if I wanted to go riding in his new car and I said sure. I jumped in the car and we picked up some cold beer and here we went. It was in the summertime. He said, "Let's drive out to Old Hickory Lake." They had just started working on Old Hickory Lake and they were just filling it up. We drove around the powder plant around Hendersonville. They used to make stuff for World War II. We stopped and picked up some more beer since we had already drunk what we bought. Back then you used to pick up beer at places you knew. He pulled off awful close to the lake. We were sitting there drinking beer and telling tales to each other. Well all at once he decided to drive. He fired that little shit up and took off flying right towards the water. I was screaming and jumping. I almost fell out of it. He went out right in the damn water. I was raising hell at him and yelled saying, "Shit you're crazy!" All at once he reached down and snatched something on the floor and here we went right into the water. I thought holy crap! Well it had a little propeller in the back of it. He was riding all over the lake. There wasn't any boats out there. Just some people fishing off the banks and they couldn't believe it. I can't remember the name of the car; I think it was a Sunbeam or something like that. You were awful close to the water on the sides. There wasn't enough space between me and the water. It came up pretty high on both sides. I thought why in the hell would a fella want this car. It wasn't a good boat either! I don't know what it was good for. It was fun, after a few beers. It was something else.

I've seen a lot of stuff that people wouldn't believe when you were born back when I was born. I have had the privilege of seeing this country really become something. I may have the privilege of seeing it go back to nothing again at the rate we are going. It ain't funny neither!

The 1950s by Karen Dodson

The 1950s was a golden age in America.

I remember wooden roller rinks, ice skating on the flooded baseball fields in the parks where we gathered on summer nights to watch a local ball game. People would sit on their front porches listening to the ball game and keep an eye on the neighborhood kids.

They put straight pipes on custom cars (chopped and channeled) to make racket. Everything was chromed under the hood (Mercury made a cool one and your date raised the hood at the drive in so it could be admired) Ten or more kids in a convertible even in the well (where the top went when down) to go riding. We usually only bought 1 gallon of gas to drive around on!

Girls would show their legs to judge who had the prettiest ones. We parked in the graveyard to drink beer. A bunch of us walking and singing the latest hit parade songs. There were pajama parties with a lot of talk of who liked which boys. We had red soles on those saddle shoes, denim jackets, and field jackets. We knew you didn't go near the pool hall as they sold reefers there or we thought they did. The local beat cop talking to us and telling us not to start smoking because boys didn't like tobacco lips. Johnny Ray singing Little White Cloud that Cried and us singing it as we walked to grade school. Spoolies, bubble beads, rolled down socks. Boys putting playing cards in the spokes of their bikes to sound like tail pipes. Crack the whip and clamp on roller skates. Was it really that long ago???? Trading cards, trading comic books. There was the green and blue screen you put over the black and white TV to have color. We turned the lights out and watched Inner Sanctum which was really scary --next to The

Wax Museum. Musical Movies, Marge and Grover Champion were favorites. Friday and Sunday we would have to go to the 10 cent movies and sit in the second row, funny we aren't all cross eyed from it! (Of course we snuck in friends through the exit door) Older kids sat in the balcony so they could "neck". Three cowboy movies and 24 cartoons kept us out of our parent's hair on weekends. A family bakery was located every two to three blocks and that would scent the neighborhood early every morning. I really miss those times!

Backfire

Me and Charlie K were down at the liquor store. We had a bad habit of drinking and standing around. Well when things were quiet we would sit there, have a drink and get to talking. Charlie carried a big ole .45 and he was always bragging about how powerful it was and how good it could shoot and everything. I had a Colt .38. It was a Texas cowboy type of .38, had a barrel that looked like a .22 rifle. I had those super bells that police had back then. They had just come out with them. It got close to closing time and we got to arguing about who had the most powerful gun. The more we argued, well the more we drank and finally we closed up and walked back to the liquor store where we had things stored in the back room. We cleared out a spot back there. I don't know why we did it. We got side by side and flipped to see who would shoot first. He won.

There was a little space in between us. We were going to shoot at the block wall to see what damage the shell would do to it. Well anybody with sense would know that was a bad move to make. When they built those block walls they used solid block or poured concrete and steel. Charlie pulled out the .45 and picked out a block and we were 20 feet from the wall. He fired and when he did, BIIIIIIIIING, came a bullet just flying and it didn't make a mark on the wall. I looked at Charlie and he turned white as a sheet. It went right between us and I thought, well shit, that wasn't too bright. He said, "Well I guess that answers it, there isn't no need"....I said, "No hold on a damn minute. You got to shoot yours and now I have to shoot mine." When I told him that his legs started shaking. I thought if I hit where he did it's bound to do the same thing again. He stood there shaking and I let him shake awhile. I aimed right at the same damn spot. I fired and all at once, the bullet came right back by us the same way. Well we didn't do that anymore. Charlie almost crapped in his britches, well me too really.

Pappy Hoots

I'm not sure that your life isn't laid out in a pattern before you are ever born because of the way my wife Karen and I met. One time we were over at Pappy Hoot's. That's where we met friends of ours, Beverly, Charlie, the Hoot's Family. The Hoot's lived down the street and they loved young people. Everybody would meet at their house and Mammy Hoots would cook and we would meet and dance and sing and do some drinking. Pappy Hoots loved young people and loved being around young people and he had a good time with us. Everybody every weekend would show up there. Things were good. Everybody liked everybody. Just to show you how funny things are. I was sitting and talking. There were two nightclubs, the Palms and Starlight on Dickerson Road. That is where everybody would go to dance on the weekends. Back then I thought I was something. I loved the Jitterbug and all of that. I got out there one Saturday Night and I knew the woman that ran the place. There was a gal out there that could really cut a rug. I asked her to dance and back then you could throw women on your side and up in there air. Well, I weighed about 140 pounds dripping wet. Well, before I got to telling the story, Karen told me to be quiet and she finished telling the rest of the story. I couldn't believe it. What happened was that I threw her from right hip to left hip and in between my legs. Well you are supposed to grab their hands as they are passing through, well I missed her hands and she went scooting across the floor and she hit the jukebox and burnt up her butt! Well the jukebox had something on it that got damaged and I ending up paying for it. She got mad and got up and left. I couldn't believe it was Karen and that was way before we ever met over there! I also can't believe how she put up with me like she did.

Those Damn Hippies by Will Dodson

Reader, imagine the environment for just a moment in the late 1960s in Hillsboro Village located in Nashville, Tennessee. My parents lived in Hillsboro Village renting a small apartment located blocks away from "Pappy Hoots" mentioned earlier. My Dad having had one too many, or par for the course for him at that time, ended up on the back porch of Pappy Hoot's barely able to stand up. Pappy came out wanting to know what the hell my Dad was doing out there at 2 AM on his porch. Pappy said, "Don't worry about it, I'll go inside and make you some coffee and sober you up a bit". When he went back inside the door swung back and hit my Dad, my dad stumbled and went right off the porch. It was a good four or five feet fall and he landed in a thorn bush. A few minutes later with a freshly brewed cup of coffee, Pappy came out and surveyed the porch.

He said, "Well that drunk sonofabitch must have wandered off!" Dad tried to speak and tried to move, but he couldn't as he was nicely tangled in the thorn bush. Pappy went back inside cussing and my Dad finally managed his way out of the thorn bush for the trek back home. I would say he was trekking back home to a worried wife but my Mom knew he was nearby but she was up all the same. She asked him what in the world had happened as he came through the door with scratches all over his face and neck. He said, "Well I was down on 21st and a van load of those damn hippies attacked me, I had to fight them off, I think one of them stabbed me!" Reader, whenever you are trying to come up with a tall tale and you are trying to make yourself appear to be riding off in the sunset, at least say you were attacked by something other than hippies.

No Hands

Well, Reader. I'm going to tell you about the time I cut off my fingers in an accident. I was working for a company in Nashville and I was on the grease rack. My job was greasing trucks, changing oil in the dumping trucks. I did a lot of spray painting. I painted just about everything you can paint. The painter that painted the trucks came down and asked my foreman if he could get me to come up and help him. I left the grease rack and went with him to help him. They had this truck that they had painted yellow. It was the truck they take out to put fuel in bulldozers in the field. They took the guard off of a compressor on the truck; they put new belts on the compressor. I looked in it and there was no gas, couldn't start. I crawled up on it. We were going to cover the front of the truck because it had been painted yellow. The tank we were going to paint black. Well they had the paint there and spray gun ready and I was finishing wrapping the front so it wouldn't get any black paint on it. There wasn't a lot of room between where the compressor was and the back of the truck and I had my hand in it and all at once that damn compressor started up. I had my hands on the belt. Well when it started up it cut my little finger plum off and it fell in a bucket of paint and cut all the rest of them and they were just hanging. It didn't hurt because I went into shock. Lord have mercy, I looked down and saw my hand with all of those fingers hanging everywhere and my thumb was gone too. I threw my hip up against the big wheel and grabbed those belts with the other hand to slow it down. It was slowly dragging my other hand in there. A mechanic came by and seen it and he jumped up there and cut everyone of those belts off where they could get me out of there. So when I got out they hauled me to the hospital. I got in there and let me tell you it was a third rate hospital. I won't name it. I got over there and couldn't get the doctor because he was on the golf course. They stuck my hand in a bowl of something and stuck me in a room, which was a linen closet. I was in shock so bad that I really wasn't hurting. A few minutes later I heard my wife asking for me. They said, "Oh he's in the operating room!" I said, "Hey!!! Come on down here!" She said, "What the hell are you doing in there!?!" I said, "This is where they put me, in the damn closet!" She got to raising hell with them and it wasn't a few minutes later the doctor came in and started working on me.

I told you all of this to show you how all of this came about. Back then you weren't covered like you are now. They fixed my hand and laid me off. I had my hand in a cast with pins in my fingers. We went home. That company laid me off but they had 3,500 employees and I was the only one they laid off. Well after coming home, I was constipated. I couldn't go to the bathroom at all. I wasn't having a fit. I told my wife, "Damn, you've got to do something, I'm dying with this hand and I can't go to the bathroom, I feel like I'm passing a bowling ball." She said, "I'm tired of hearing you complain." She fixed a big ole milkshake of Milk of Magnesia or something and I drank it all. She forgot about giving me that stuff. She said, "Well you are laid off and we'll just go up to momma's in Wisconsin." We had a Volkswagen Beetle and believe it or not they go anywhere, I bet they would drive on water if you had it in a lake. But anyways, we forgot about that dose of medicine. We had our baby son with us. We took off and she was doing all the driving. We got up to Indiana and all at once a pain hit me and I said, "Lord have mercy! Pull over, I've got to go!" Well it got to snowing where you couldn't see and the highway wasn't cleared good. I couldn't hold it any longer and I crapped in my britches. We pulled in a service station. I ran into that bathroom. I almost never got my britches down. I finally got them down. I took my drawers and cut them off with a pocket knife and threw them away. I got up and washed up as best as I could. I couldn't get my britches back up. I thought well I will go to the car and get my wife to button them up. I started out across the lot and it had hell it had got icy. All at once both of my feet went straight up in the damn air and the only thing that hit the ground first was my head and I fell and them britches came down on me like a window shade. There I was butt naked crying. I got to crying, hell I was hurting and I cried like a baby. The guy that owned the service station never laughed or nothing. He walked over and asked what in the world was wrong. I said, "The whole damn world is against me brother." He said, "How bad are you hurt?" I said, "I can't be no damn worse than I am. I cut all my fingers off." He looked down there and I was butt naked. "What in the world has happened?" he said. I told him, "I shit in my britches because she didn't get me in here fast enough, I ain't got but one hand and couldn't get my britches up, I cut my drawers off and threw them away, I cleaned up as best I could in there and I can't button my britches." He said, "Well let me tell you something son. I've been here thirty years and had to do just about everything there was but I ain't never had to help a man put his britches on." It was funny now but it wasn't then. He never laughed. He told me, "I'll help you up and get behind you and I'll button up your britches, don't worry about that mess in there, I'll get that cleaned up because I feel sorry for you." He helped me to the car. I told my wife, "I don't give a shit what happens, the next damn town we come by, I'm getting some jogging pants that I can pull up and down. If I have to go again, you just stop and I'll just wash my butt in the snow." Well I did, we had to stop three or four times. I bet that man told everybody that story.

Joe Knows Pantyhose

I'll tell you about the time Joe Namath won the Super bowl with the Jets. He told about wearing women's pantyhose to keep warm in that cold New York weather. This ole boy we hung out with got mad about Joe Namath and them hose and said he's crazy and must be gay. He got to carrying on. I said, oh Lord there is nothing wrong with that, he did that to keep warm. Well he went wild.

Well it was around Christmas and we were going to Bellevue to one of those subdivisions to a party. Well my buddy that raised Cain about Joe Namath was there. I told my wife to leave a pair of those pantyhose out. I was going to put them on and go over there and aggravate him. I got my britches on and slipped on those pantyhose. I didn't think anything about it and went out and get in the car. When I turned out of the driveway onto Highway 100 there were a bunch of State troopers out there checking everybody. Traffic was jammed up. I slowed down and tried to reach in my back pocket to try and get my license out and those damn pantyhose were so tight I couldn't get my hand in there to get my wallet. While I was doing that I had the car slowly moving ahead and had my leg stretched out where I could get my wallet. I bumped into the car ahead of me and the State Trooper was there and I bumped him. I cut the engine off and he looked back at me and came back and said "Sir are you drinking?" I said, "No Sir." He said, "Why did you bump that car?" I said, "Well I was trying to get my wallet out." He said, "Get out of the car." I said, "Do I got to?" He said, "Yeah you got to, get out of that damn car!" I pulled out of the car and there I was with those pantyhose stretched over my pants. He said, "What in the world?" I said, "You ain't going to believe this but I've got to tell you something." He said, "Yeah I reckon you better." I said, "I put these on as a joke to a fella at a party. I put these on because he carried on about Joe Namath." He said, "I tell you what, I believe you need to get in the car and go on!"

Dancing Dula

At my son's wedding, my wife and I were dancing to the music. One of his coworkers said that I had soul. Well, you know where that came from? When I was out at TIS, there were dances held at the gym on the basketball floor. All the girls came around wanting us to dance with them and we were young and we thought it was sissy like. So we didn't do it. When I got in boot camp and got to go out, we would go in a place and there were all these gals wanting to dance. I couldn't' dance and hell they didn't hang around with me, they were gone. If a fella couldn't dance, he didn't get any dates. Boy, I was getting down in the dumps, I thought, Lord this isn't going to get it. So I went and signed up for Arthur Murray in a hurry. I wasn't making a lot of money at the time, so they let me pay as I went. They give you a teacher and she teaches you to two step and double dip. I thought, boy, look out Hollywood, here I come. Now California was strict when you were underage and wanting to get into these joints. They would run you off. I was too young to legally drink. But, we went anyways, I would ask a girl to dance and I was tickled to death. We would get up there and I would start that square dancing and she would take a look at me and laugh. I thought, holy crap, what in the world have I done. So I went back onto the ship. We had a black man on our ship named Dula. He and I would have to scrape paint and chip. On these ships, they would make you chip the paint where there was a rust spot, put chromade on it or redlead. Dula could take a chipper and beat on that side of that ship and sing and dance while he was doing it. When he was on a scaffold on the side, he would do the fancy stepping while he was working. Well, I got him to the side and told him, "Man Dula, I've got to learn how to dance." He said, "Hell I can't dance with you, we'd get killed if anybody seen us!" So we would sneak off to the engine room, where nobody was around, and he worked on teaching me how to dance. He said, "You've got to have rhythm and get the feeling." This is where I found my love for music. Ella Fitzgerald, Nat King Cole were my favorites. You remember I met her and got her autograph, that's another story, but God it was like talking to an angel. Nat King Cole, if it wasn't for him, I would have never gotten any dates! But anyways, Dula got to showing me the steps. I actually learnt how to dance from Dula. That is where the soul came from. I can hear a song now and my blood just jumps with it. If I was born today, even as bow legged and knock kneed as I am, I would have been a hell of a break dancer! I would give anything to dance like the kids today. I love dancing and I love good soul music. I like Country Music today as well. If you really want to give credit to where credit is due, Elvis isn't the King of Rock and Roll. The King is Little Richard. If it wasn't for the black beat, you wouldn't have the rhythm and the dancing you have today. You can't dance to "She'll Be Coming Around the Mountain" and it's hard to break dance to "Old Speckled Bird"! Well, onto other subjects.

Indian Rasslin'

You ever know that one single person in your life that can get you in the most trouble. Well I sure did, Reader. That person was Ray. He could get me in a hell of a fix in no time. A short order cook for trouble.

You see Ray was older than me and was married. I was about 16 years old and in the National Guard. One day at Fort Campbell, in Clarksville I was smoking a cigarette. You see, Reader, we were in the Guard at this time. Well I was finishing a cigarette and threw it on the ground and Ray told me, "You know you're not supposed to throw cigarette butts out on the grounds?" I said, "The hell with that, I can do what I want to." Right then I realized a sergeant was standing right behind me. Ray had set me up. That sonofabitch. The sergeant said, "Pick that butt up and come with me son." Well I didn't know what he was about to do. He took me over to an MP and informed him that I was to give that cigarette a full military burial. With shovel in hand I spent hours digging a 6 ft by 6ft grave to bury my cigarette butt. I went looking for Ray after that but he was nowhere to be found.

Ray had a wife that didn't like me much. I don't know why, but she didn't. He'd get drunk and I would drive him home and she'd blame me for what he did. Well one night I was driving him home. You know because I was one of those drinkers that still thought I could drive better then the best teetotaler out there. So when I turned the corner I saw her standing there waiting, arms crossed and reading to jump my case. Well Reader, I didn't feel like having my case jumped so as I neared the house he opened the door and got out and I never stopped, I kept the car going. Only problem was he didn't make it all the way out and I was dragging him in front of his house and more importantly in front of his wife. I'm not sure why she never liked me much. Well, Reader, I can tell this story, because I'm part Cherokee. So don't take any offense to the story I'm about to tell. Ray and I walked into a bar up in Nashville and I threw a little money on the bar for drinks and went on to the back to the bathroom. Well when I got back the biggest Indian I've ever seen was standing there over my money, which was laying on the bar. I went to ask about my beer and told the bartender I had laid the money down. The big ole Indian looked at me and told me, "That's my money". I said, "The hell it is." Reader, I thought my life was over. I didn't know Indians got this big. He told me, "You aren't taking it." I said "The hell I'm not!" Right before the devil had me Ray came around the corner and sized that Indian up (even though he was half the Indian's size) and said, "You're an Indian aren't ya?" The big guy looked him up and down and said, "Yeah, I am, what about it?" "Well, do you rassle?", Ray said. The Indian was taken aback and then started laughing, bought a round for us and then had to leave. I never in my life.

Toys Today and Yesterday

Talking about toys. Well my son had plenty of He-man and Hotwheels. Well, I was thinking of things we had as kids. We used to take the pop tops on beer cans and make chains out of them and way before that we would make chains out of dandelions and that is where I got my other nickname "June bug". I would take a piece of thread and spend hours flying June bugs. You could take a big ole beetle and tie a thread to its leg and he would fly around and around. I guess today, that would be cruelty. The best toy I remember was when I was a kid in Lenoir City. An uncle of mine there could whittle and make anything. He would make birdhouses that were detailed with windows, doors, swings, and little rocking chairs. He could take a pocketknife and make anything. If he was alive today, he would make a fortune, I never saw anything like it. I don't know if you ever heard about rat killings, but, we used to do a lot of that. You could take a Y shaped limb out of a tree and peel the bark off it and make a good sling shot. Way back then, the old inner tubes were made out of real rubber and they would stretch. Well you take that rubber and those flip stock and cut you a tongue out of an old shoe and you could make a pocket to hold your rock or marble.

I was good shooting marbles. I came in third place shooting marbles. My best shooting ball was a steel ball, but you couldn't use that in a contest. I would use an extra large logroller. It was a big marble. I could really clear out a circle of marbles. You make a big circle and you put the marbles in the middle and you start shooting them. Kinda like shooting pool. I could get into a barn and take out a bunch of pigeons with the marbles. We would eat them. Well, my uncle whittled me out a gun and it looked something like a carbine. It was a nice one. He made a chamber on it and a trigger that would cock on it. He used rubber bands where I could stretch it. I could put a tin penny nail in that thing and it was accurate. I would give anything to have it today. I could have made a fortune with it. I would kill rats with it. The corn that fed those chickens attracted the rats. They would come around the outhouse too and I would sit back and pop them. I got where I was pretty good with it. We had the gun, the flip stock and we would take a cane and make a plunger and whittle it out and use those berries and you could make a pop gun and shoot berries at each other. We also had stickball.

When I was out at TIS they had a game out there that we used to play cork. You could take a cork and you could put tape around it. The more tape you put around it, the heavier it got and the faster you could throw it. You could take a cork and hold it between your thumb and two fingers. There were different ways you could throw it. You could put a curve on it. You could have an incurve, an outcurve, a drop, any throw. You wouldn't believe the throws you could make. You had a pitcher and catcher and hitter. Sometimes if you were playing with a heavy cork, you would have a guy in the outfield to catch it. If you struck it and missed three times you were out. You would be surprised; you would really have to have patience to hit that cork. Some people got good at it. Red Galler out there that used to be the coach, he was one of the best cork players out there. He could smack the fool out of that cork. What you use for a bat is a broomstick or mop handle. You would stand there and you had to have a good eye for that cork. That was one of the games we played.

We had different games we would play. We would sneak down to the barn at night and have cow pie fights. That doesn't sound like fun, but it was. You would wait until it was dark and I found out if you got a stack of them and hid them, then you could lay down with a stack of them and when somebody came by, you could really zing them with them.

Well sometimes they were really mushy on the inside and you would really have to bathe when you got back. We also had corncob fights. I almost lost an eye doing that. I quit that after a guy hit me with one when I peeked around the corner of the barn. That wasn't as much fun.

I would listen to Randy's Record Mart. That was the music that people listened to. You could get all of the good black soul music on it. That was one of my favorite sets. I played them on a radio that a fella made for me. I can't tell you how he made it, but it was really good, it was the closest thing to a radio that I had. I would lay there at night with my head under the pillow listening to it. The toys we had weren't much, there wasn't any Pac man or any of that stuff. We would have went wild if we had had Nintendos, computers, Playstations, etc.

"Chick" Dodson (back row far left), San Diego 1950

Tennessee Chicken Quotes

"My wife was a poor man's Martha Stewart. She could do anything."

"I can't believe you can get a picture through a wire from way off or from a satellite. The television is one of the biggest marvels I've ever seen. Also air conditioning is incredible. Things that you take for granted everyday such as television and air conditioning."

"People today take pills and talk about their depression. What's depression? Depression didn't exist when I was little, or at least we didn't know what depression was, we knew what hungry was."

"I don't know why everybody talks about radios back in the 30s. We didn't have any radio"

"Well, Tennessee Chicken, they had radios in the 30s!"

"Yeah, you try plugging a radio into a kerosene lamp!"

Kitchen Table

I own one of the most famous tables in the country. If that table could talk and tell you who sat it, you wouldn't believe it. There have been Chiefs of Police, cops, thugs, priests, and money people in Nashville, everybody sitting at that table at one time or another. That table came out of an undisclosed location in Nashville. I won't tell you exactly where, but there may or may not have been mafia at that table. In fact, a lot of mobsters sat at that table. I was sitting there the other day and thinking about all the folks that have sat there. There has been a fortune on that table.

I'll just call the previous owner "P". Well P, who owned the table, had a deep freeze with little brown sacks with $5,000 in each sack and it was packed to the brim. He had property all over Nashville and had one of the biggest bootlegging operations going on. There was a Jew, who wanted to borrow money from P. I don't know if there was interest, I'm sure there was. This guy wanted to open a business. He borrowed one sack of money and he went up town and opened an Army & Navy store in a long deep room. He had shelves in there stocked well with uniforms and everything looked nice. Back on the back he had boxes and on each one he had ribbons and medals and some of them wouldn't have one or two pieces. It looked like the store was really stocked, but it wasn't. When somebody would order something, he would have to delay and even pull stuff out of the window. The man ended up buying three rental places in Knoxville, Tennessee and he made all kinds of money.

I used to hang out at P's house and told him all about my travels to Italy.

An Ugly Chic(k)a

My wife and I went on one of those boat rides (on a cruise ship). We were somewhere down in the Caribbean. They had a party on the fan tail. Well my wife went on up and I said there was something I wanted to do. I bought me a great big ole straw hat in Cozumel. Well I was trucking along, wearing that hat and I wasn't listening to what was going on. There were five women in a group and there was a whole bunch of grooms. When I walked up with that hat on these gals ran up to me and said, "We are picking you!" I said, "Picking me for what?" They said, "You are going to be ours and we have to dress you up like a woman to enter into a contest." I said, "Well that sounds ok to me." They were five of the prettiest women I had ever seen in my life! Well my wife was in another group and she had run a beauty shop for years and was ready to doll some man up for the competition. Well these girls took me back to their room and they painted my fingernails and did a bunch of stuff to me. Well I had a mustache. They picked some kind of bathing suit that I barely fit in. I got the ugliest legs you've ever seen with double jointed knees and believe me when I say that, because I won the ugliest legs contest in Nashville and that's when we had about 300,000 living there at the time. There I was in that outfit and I was, I was pitiful looking. They were tickled to death. We got back up there and they got us up on stage and they had cards they would give you. You had to repeat what that card said. There were about eight of us dressed as women. Each one got up there and read their card and did a little dance. My card said, "I am Wanda Valdez, I grind coffee so fine." I said it and shook my fanny. They were all roaring with laughter. Well there was this one fella that got up and he was the prettiest fella I ever laid eyes on and could really dance, come to find out he was gay. He had his own dress so the competition wasn't fair. My wife had fixed his hair up really pretty. He got first and I got second but what made it funny was when it was all over with I was going to go back and change. This lady came running up and asked for me and said, "Wait Wanda, come back and meet my family." I said, "What do you mean?" She said, "Grandma wants to see you." I said, "Well didn't grandma see enough of me?" She said, "We are the Valdez family and grandma wants to meet you." I couldn't believe it. Well, the gals got me back to the room and I got my clothes. I asked if they had any fingernail polish remover and they didn't have any. Well the next day when I went to breakfast these guys would see that fingernail polish and back off and it was getting to me. I went to the store and nobody had any. I told my wife, "Hell, everybody thinks I'm gay on this ship!" Finally we got sandpaper and sanded it and that was a job. But all in all it was real nice meeting the Valdez family!

A Broken Heart

They say God is great and God is good. God gives us life and he gives us death. He brings us into this World and he takes us out. There is one thing that there ain't nothing on the earth can take care of and that is memory. Memory of someone that passes away and you have to live without them. Memory can be painful and it's long lasting and you can't get away from it. There is no way of forgetting it. Scientists and doctors say there is no such thing as a broken heart. They are wrong. There may not be a broken heart that you can catch on an x-ray or a negative. There is an unseen heart that never keeps bleeding.

True Love by Will Dodson

There have been a great many songs, books, and movies dedicated to love stories and all are timeless in their own way. One love story that will never be known but is none the lesser in power, feeling, or dedication than the great love stories of all time is the love story between my Mom and Dad.

After the Korean War, my father fell into a dark period of alcoholism and loneliness. In the 1950s and 1960s, he worked various jobs from running a printing press to painting houses and then to running a liquor store. He used alcohol as a crutch to get by and to deal with the painful memories that he carried from childhood and the Korean War. My Dad met my Mom in the late 1960s, through a mutual friend, at the home of Pappy Hoots, who is mentioned earlier in this book. At that point in his life, my Dad was heading on a path towards destruction and without the love and intercession on behalf of my Mom, I wouldn't be here today and writing this book with my Dad. My mom took care of my Dad making sure all facets of his life were taken care of, including his health. She cooked for him and he gained back weight and she cut down on his drinking and his smoking and his overall health improved. Their companionship would last for over forty years.

In 2006, my Mom started showing signs of the early stages of Amyotrophic Lateral Sclerosis (ALS), otherwise known as "Lou Gehrig's Disease". The initial signs were a dragging of her right foot and, at that time, it was thought that this was the cause of a compressed disc in her back, affecting the nerve in her leg. Eventually, paralysis set in on both her right leg and eventually her left leg. Reader, if you have been confronted with a terminal disease it is a frightening time for everyone involved, not just the victim. My Mom and Dad, in their typical style, fought this terrible disease together. They were both children of the Great Depression and fighters, having lived through that time; they both knew how to make the most out of a rough situation. As my Mom's condition worsened and she had difficulty taking care of the basic necessities such as using the bathroom and feeding herself, my Dad was by her side every moment and took care of every detail even when his own health was declining. A good family friend helped build a ramp to the back door of the house, and other friends showed up and took care of this task or that task. Everyone started pitching in to help the woman, who helped so many during her life. If one of my Mom's friends came on hard times, she would hand them a check and never ask for anything back. She would stop by and bring groceries to someone, who couldn't afford food or help someone who was going through a rough spell. Our family is small and where we didn't have any relatives nearby. We had friends, who became like family and stuck together to support my Mom. The ALS Association in Tennessee provided great support to my family during this dark time. My Mom saved my Dad's life when they first got married. He was an alcoholic and as he says would have drank himself to death. My Mom stopped that habit and changed his life around. Dad took care of her night and day and never left her side through the good fight. In May of 2011, my Mom was admitted to St. Thomas Hospital and we all knew it would be the last trip. My Dad sat by her side for three days straight and would not leave her for a moment. Mom bravely fought ALS, and she was surrounded by friends and family in her last moments on this Earth. While the passing of my Mom is the most difficult moment I have ever experienced thus far in my life, I know it was much more difficult for my Dad. We both held her hands as the host of angels took her to her eternal rest and in my sincerest hope and faith to a grand reunion with all of those loved ones, who passed on before. My Dad stood by her the entire time. It was my Mom, who saved my Dad's life and took care of him through his dark times and it was my Dad, who took care of my Mom and walked with her through her dark times to eternal life. A greater love story could never be told and writing it does not do it justice. Reader, I know that one day my father will pass and I know that one day I will follow and I believe with all my heart that upon that day my parents will be waiting with all my missed loved ones and our Lord for me to partake in that eternal life. The eternal life that awaits us all on the other side of our reality, that place that is so profound and that while we are making our way through this life journey on Earth, indeed we long to be there again.

Karen and Chick Dodson, November 11, 2006

80 Year Old Paratrooper

On August 7, 2011 my Dad turned 80 years old. 80 years of life that we can hardly imagine. The history he had lived through and the changes he saw with his own two eyes (remarkable he still had both as he doesn't have all his fingers, but that's saved for Tennessee Chicken, Vol. II). My Dad wanted to mark these 80 grand (and grand is sometimes a questionable word) years with a leap from a perfectly good airplane. So, after a number of setbacks in August, we finally got him signed up to jump with an outfit in Waverly, TN. It was a beautiful September day with not a cloud in the sky and it was a perfect day to jump out of a perfectly good airplane. My wife's cousin, Jeanne, made the jump with him. Reader, I am only 32 years old at the writing of this book and have no want, need, or inclination to jump, but that didn't stop cousin Jeanne and Dad. His bravery never ceases to amaze me. Dad made his jump with a solider from Fort Campbell as his instructor. How fitting for a Korean vet to jump with America's finest. This made jump number one for Dad but jump 1,000 for the paratrooper. As Dad floated back to Earth, I remarked to myself how this man had overcome so many things in his life and could still carry forward with a smile.

Conclusion

Well reader, this is the end of Tennessee Chicken's stories for now, unless he remembers a few more that we can stick in this book! The stories get better and a little longer every time he tells them!

My Dad has lived through 13 presidents, been run over by a Hudson, had a grenade explode behind him in Korea, had fingers and a thumb cutoff, been shot at, fallen off multiple buildings, been attacked by a pit bull and a wild hog, had a wasp's nest fall in his mouth and he has survived. His guardian angel must be one broken down, tired, worn down, dragging, unable to fly angel at this point! He has lived an adventurous life. In fact, at times it was probably too adventurous. He has seen this country grow from the dismal days when he came into this world and saw poverty at some of its worse to a country where most people have enough to eat and complain if there is no wireless internet! He lived on the streets, at times in cardboard boxes and bathed in the creeks and rivers of Tennessee. He lived in the orphanage and made friends along the way. He survived freezing nights in Korea where his toes were frostbitten and he survived war. He overcame alcoholism and found my mother, who saved his life. He met famous folks along the way and lived through the 1950s, seeing the adoption of items we take for granted today such as television and air-conditioning. Dad has been around the world twice and he has met all kinds of people along the way. He loves this country and he loves our servicemen. He is a true American patriot. We hope this book gave you some laughs along the way and above all we hope that it gives you hope in your life.

As I said at the beginning of this book, Someone is always watching over you and leading you through your own individual set of adventures. Life is truly what you make it to be and we hope this book provided you with some entertainment and comfort in your life.

Chick's 80th Birthday Skydive